CHAMPION'S HANDBOOK

Meteoric Guide for Meteoric Success

notionpress
.com

CHAMPION'S HANDBOOK

Meteoric Guide for Meteoric Success

Rishank Jhavar

notionpress.com

Notion Press

Old No. 38, New No. 6

McNichols Road, Chetpet

Chennai - 600 031

First Published by Notion Press 2015

ISBN: 978-93-52062-47-8

To war,

To peace.

Foreword

I remember someone famous once remarked that the sign of a great book is that you want to call up the author as a friend and tell him he wrote a great book. When I read that quote, I just smiled. I had felt that way many times, and I am sure many readers know that feeling. But then, the author being dead is an issue often. So you can imagine what I felt the day when my friend and the author of this book actually told me that he wrote it. But before that, one of those anecdotes without which no foreword is complete.

You have the book in your hands, so it might be safe to assume that you can be bothered with an incident (and that's putting it mildly) or two about the man in whose brain it all began. I remembered the first time I noticed him. He was being stripped of his captaincy for not doing history homework. I am sure till date that he mouthed some religious words and let the incident go. I remember reading classics of literature together with him, and I also remember all the mistakes, the highs and the lows that he had. But there's nothing unique in that, every boy has them. You see, what makes it all special is that not everyone goes and pens down a book about it. Many want to, but they do not, and cannot. To say that we grew up together wouldn't be exaggerating, and to say that there was a writer always inside him wanting to come out wouldn't be opportunistic. He used to actually write a lot, and I remember that people used to like his poems and ask for more, like subscribing to a blog or a feed. Things have clearly taken a turn for better, and what I can notice reading the book is, it is about a journey, a change, a transition. Just as the butterfly is proof that we can overcome difficulties and become something beautiful, the book is a symbol of that.

The only journey is the one within, as Rilke once remarked, and that sentiment is echoed through the book. While reading self-help books, a specific age group often feels that the ideas purported and advice given is obsolete and has lost its relevance.

The battle of youth and age is one in which everyone changes sides, and this book was written especially with the younger, currently-in-developing-stage-youngsters (though those still young at heart are welcome too, age is just a state of mind, as Cicero said).

This neo-motivation, let's call it, provides for quite an interesting twist on some old as time topics like anger, sloth, and hope among others. The aim of this book is not to give you help, but to give you the ability to help yourself, much like teaching a man how to fish, rather than giving him the fish. It promises to be poignant, realistic, and effective, so that we may become something bigger than we think we can be. The Poet of all America, Walt Whitman wrote in his Song of Myself "behold I do not give lectures or charity… when I give, I give myself"

In the name of the best in all of us.

Parth Khare

Preface

There is a reason why boxing is a sport that gives you that little rush of adrenaline. The idea of two men, battling with only their fists becomes an easy stand in for the life struggles of every man. And there is no better story that paraphrases this sport's nature than James J. Braddock's.

Braddock lost 16 of the 26 fights in his initial career. He was scoffed at by the audience. He broke his right hand and retired. He lost all the money he had. He was ridiculed everywhere.

He had no educational qualification, so no work. He had no connections, nothing hidden up his sleeve. He was stamped a loser. The loser.

But even losers have to do something for their bread. For their families. He was no different. He walked 10–15 miles a day to feed his family; taking up whatever job he was given. One day, he somehow landed a bout against a strong boxer, John Griffin. He was intended to be a mere stepping stone in Griffin's career. Everyone already saw the clear winner in Griffin.

They were waiting for his early knockout win. They were waiting for the fight to end in third or fourth round. And they were right. The fight did end in the third round. But it wasn't Griffin who won. It was the loser who won.

Bit by bit, he worked his way towards the top. All around him, there were people biting the dust. But he knew the only way to zip his loudmouthed critics was one; just one. The greatest prize of them all. The World Heavyweight Championship title. The defeat of the great Max Baer.

He was still considered frail and inferior. And this led to Baer's agents hand picking him for the title shot.

The miracle happened. On June 13, 1935, James J. Braddock, the loser, knocked Baer out by 10–1 to become one of the greatest athlete to grace the game; ever.

Feeling inspired? No? If yes, you're missing the entire point. This story isn't here to inspire you or to give you some goose bumps; no. There are millions of other inspirational stories and movies out there (even this story was turned into a flick some years back). It is here to make it clear to you that everybody loves underdogs. Why? Universal reasoning answers this question as 'We all root for thrills and unexpected stuff, and so the victories of the underdogs excite us so much that we go ecstatic.' Well that is pretty heavy.

First of all, why are we talking about underdogs? Shouldn't we get straightaway to business and talk about being a champion? That is what this book is all about, isn't it? *Motivating.* That is why it began with a success story! Nope. First of all, success stories are not merely meant to pump you up with motivation, they are also meant to make you understand those small things in life that champions carry. So, again, why are we talking about underdogs here? Because every champion begins as one. You are beginning as one. Don't believe this?

Well, if you have picked this book up, you are probably someone who really wants to succeed in life. You are probably someone, who, when around six or seven year old, were expected to make a mark in the world. You were a prodigy in the eyes of your parents, weren't you? And then, you grew up. And growing up, you started failing. You started failing in small and big things in your life. Not even your parents, siblings or even you could identify what happened.

Or probably you are the other kind. If you can read this line, you have all the brains, all the potential in yourself. But the problem is that you are not able to utilize your potential.

Maybe you consider yourself as nothing, but you have picked this book up, so you have a slight desire to become a successful person, right?

You may fall in any of the categories stated above, or any other. But there is one common link: you have a desire, a burning desire to grab success and show the world who you are. You have a great desire to spit on the faces of those who questioned your potential. And you have a great desire to become a champion. That is the very reason why you are an underdog.

The feeling of being an underdog is visibly dry and uncomfortable. Underdogs start repelling people, people start repelling them, they go alone, think of everything they have lost in their lives, think of the world mocking them, and so on. But then they do something that makes people shut their mouth. They spit on the faces of their critics. They outshine everyone. Let us break things down simply. Why do we have an affinity for the underdog stories?

Wikipedia, on the definition of underdog says: 'An "underdog" is a person or group in a competition, usually in sports and creative works, who is popularly expected to lose.' Removing excess words, it simply means the person who has some disadvantage in a competition. Just like we all think we have in our lives.

We all represent underdogs. We know we are one of them. We know we have faced something similar. We know we can be successful, we know that we can become a champion. We also know that only those who are deserving will win. You must have used crayons when you were young. Do you remember that which was the least used and considered most worthless crayon in the box? White crayon. Underdogs are the white crayons. People underrate them, say that they suck, but then time comes and white crayons become the ones to create masterpieces.

This leads to a great understanding of what our brain wants and how it knows about its possibilities. It clearly highlights the fact that your brain has those things that can make you stand out as a champion. Uncovering them is the key. There is a possibility in each one of us to become a champion, if we are willing. And there, ladies and gentlemen, goes the point of this book.

You may have many goals, or you may have one single goal in life. Your goal may be something that you can define, maybe not. In any case, just remember to keep that goal in your brain while reading, because it will be addressed throughout the book. Even if you don't have a clear goal, no problem. Keep the blurry goal of being a champion, or being successful in your mind. By the end of the book, you will find everything sorted out.

Before we begin, we need to talk about a term. We need to talk about the word this entire book is based upon so that we do not get confused later. When we talk about the word 'Champion', we are generally inclined towards perceiving it as a term in sports terminology. But champions aren't merely 'proficient in sports' and all that. The word champion is derived from a Medieval Latin campio, which means 'fighter'. Its dictionary meaning goes, a person who has surpassed all rivals in competition.

Champions are the ones who have surpassed everyone they know in their life. It would be foolishness to relate the word champion to sports. An even more absurd thing would be if we call the term champion synonymous to the word winners. Champions are not mere winners; they are much more than that. They are not limited to a subject, or a thing. They have no limits. They are invincible in any sphere they want to be in. They begin as an underdog. Just like you.

This book will turn bizarre at some points. Sometimes you will be referred to as a champion. The other times you will be referred to as someone on the path to become a champion. Do not, do not get confused.

The reasoning behind this is that you have everything, everything to become what you desire. Many have everything they need to become a champion. They just don't think and discover those things. Now that is exactly where this book will help you. It will aid you in discovering things what others ignore. You are already a champion; you just need to discover it.

The chapters following this will mark the beginning of your journey. Remember that every single chapter is written to uncover the qualities which you already have. Just follow that age old golden rule: Read, think, follow. Oh, and don't expect this book to sum up in a paragraph or two. Read every single word, and put your own brain and your own thinking behind everything written.

So, hello underdog. You are someone great, and better than the others. Because people don't know about your true strength. Because they don't know your power. Because they are mere mortals and you are someone walking towards the path of becoming a champion.

Acknowledgements

This book isn't written *just* by me. When I started working on this book, I was a simple 19-year-old guy who just read stuff and knew some things about the world. But merely *knowing* about things doesn't count. You need experiences and worldly knowledge to write a motivational book. And that was provided to me by some of the most incredible people in my life.

To the almighty one up there.

To war, the one inside me.

My amazing parents, the reason of my being, for whom 'thanks' is a very, very small word.

My brother, who should actually be given all of the royalty I'll get from this book. He's the guy I've always looked up to, learned everything from. On top of all that, he gave me a great sister I never had before, in the form of my sister-in-law.

Bauji-Maa. Out of all great traits Bauji had, one of us in the family *had* to inherit the 'writing gene'. I am glad that person is me.

Nanaji-Naniji, who taught me a lot of things about this strange little thing called life.

Shreyas Sarasan and Parth Khare. Respect.

My entire family, who were more excited than me for this book.

Naman bhaiya, who provided all the valuable suggestions.

Abhishek, thanks for being there, from high school to college (damn it, stop following me dude). Chetan, Harshdeep, Chirag and Chaitanya. I would have been SCREWED in college if you weren't there. Also, Saransh, Tunnu and the entire 'Journey' film crew, you all are crazily awesome.

People like Ashi di, Archan bhaiya, Rahul, everyone, who were with me in different stages of life.

Kshitij, technically my cousin; actually my roommate. Dear reader, as you're reading this, it is highly likely that we're playing some co-op game on my Xbox.

Four of my sisters, Saky, Srishti, Mahwish and Ananya, who show that you don't really need blood relations for a bond as strong.

Mr. I.T. George, Mrs. Vineeta D'cruz, Mrs. Nina Hemraj, Mrs. Rajkumari Seth and Mrs. Kawaljeet Tuteja. Mrs. D'cruz never taught me, but was probably the first person who made me believe that I can write. Mr. George and Mrs. Hemraj are the reason I am able to form coherent sentences in English. Mrs. Rajkumari Seth and Mrs. Tuteja are the reason I know at least a decent bit about the world. Mr. Deshbir Singh and Mr. Amitava Saraswati as well, for helping me find out PCM wasn't really my cup of tea.

Everyone who have worked on this book at Notion Press, you all have been really supportive

I know that I am missing out on a lot of names, but the ones I missed out know that they have as much contribution to this book as I have. So, thank you everyone.

The guy with a first name that has no meaning,

Rishank Jhavar

Contents

Anger and Pain

At some point in life, during something that can be called a 'philosophical hangover' (the smarter ones call it an *existential crisis*), amongst many questions about life, you must have involuntarily asked yourself this one: 'What is the best feeling in the world?' The answer must have depended on your state at that time. Love, satisfaction, respect - there are many things. But let me ask you something different. What is the most productive feeling in the world?

What feeling leaves you satisfied? What feeling inspired legends to do something that made them immortal? What feeling lifts you up? What feeling forces you to overcome all odds to win? What feeling differentiates champions from the ordinary?

The answer is not in finding the ultimate feeling or in perplexing philosophies. It is just that one, simple, everyday feeling. The feeling we cannot escape. *La cólera*. Anger. Don't believe it? Okay. Let me pose as a smartass and put forward a theory. Science believes there are three major parts of the brain. The cerebrum, cerebellum and brain stem. I believe there are four. The fourth one is invisible, and it's called the anger repository.

And then there are terms like anger capacity and anger input or output. Let us consider anger's physical state as liquid. Some have a tendency to fill the anger; some have a tendency to spill the anger. The latter are mortals, spilling the anger everywhere. The aforementioned become legends.

But anger isn't a good trait, right? It is right up there on the list of *things that can destroy you*, or the list of *forbidden feelings*. Once, my teacher was blabbering about how classics like The Godfather and The Fountainhead were just meant to please readers and the 'values' they taught had no implementation strength. I corrected him, much to his annoyance. He wanted a concrete reason of how egoism, anger and other *sins* contributed towards a person's success. I explained it to him in one simple line what these classics meant. "*Every such value or sin, though apparently bad; can create wonders if they are used and utilized.*"

Of course he did not get me and I was thrown out of class for arguing. But it is simple. Do you get angry? Use that anger. Use it to prove to those people who made you angry. Or to prove to those things which made you angry. How? Heard of chainsaw? A chainsaw can be used to either chop someone's head off, or to harvest wood. Ditto, with anger. Either you can destroy yourself with it, or you can build yourself.

Let us talk about someone we know. He was pretty much a normal guy with an interest in automobiles and stuff. He had a great set of skills as well. He gave a job interview at Toyota Motors, but was turned down and this made him jobless for quite some time. It made him frustrated and angry but he held on and channeled his anger into designing scooters. Time passed and he started designing motorbikes. It blew up. Fast forward some years, and he was the proud owner of his company which he turned into a billion-dollar multinational that produced bestselling motorcycles. His engineering and marketing skills resulted in his motorcycles outselling Triumph and Harley-Davidson in their respective home markets. Toyota, the company which rejected him, didn't even come close. His name is Soichiro Honda, the guy who established Honda Motor Company Limited. Among his employees, he was known as "Mr. Thunderstorm". He got this nickname for his outbursts. Honda was loved, yet was feared because of his wrath. But it was his anger that took his company to greater heights.

In life, at every other instant you'll find people laughing at you for your small failures. Most of them will be your relatives or people you know. You will find people making you angry. What a champion does is that he glances at them, remembers their faces, smiles, and looks back at that stage in life from a more prosperous stage - a stage where he will be standing with his hands held high, and the people who laughed at him right at his feet begging for forgiveness.

That is the power anger hands you. It has moved people, nations and the world. It has put people in places they could not have imagined. It has helped people win everything. Do you know what the best part is? It is there: right in your fist. Hold it. Keep filling the anger repository.

You definitely know of Michael Jordan. He was left out of his high school's basketball team. The reason? He was 5'9. Other basketball players made fun of his height, and he was ridiculed. One day, he decided to shut their mouths. He kept filling in the anger, and gave his all to practice. He shot up to 6'3, and today, he is one of the greatest basketball players in the history of the game.

Oprah Winfrey. You know her, right? One of the greatest television personalities ever (and one of the richest women in the world), she was always fired from her jobs and was *declared* unfit for television. People laughed at her, and made fun of her looks. But she held on, never wasted *any* anger. Today? She is dubbed as the most influential woman in the world. And the channels who rejected her are the ones running after her for endorsements and interviews.

Maybe you're still skeptical about using anger as a weapon. Tell me something: When you're angry, does counting to ten help you? Drinking water? Meditation? Deep breaths? Eating? Internet forums and anger management write-ups are meant to mislead you. They'll show you wonderful and yet futile steps to throw away your anger. The newspaper articles will do the same. But tell me something, honestly. Can you do the stuff they say? No. Maybe you'll try some of them and end up wasting several minutes of your life.

Now tell me, why are humans pre-equipped with anger? Let your phone battery discharge for a day. Dumbest question ever: What will happen? "It'll turn off." Why? "Because there is no energy supply." Anger works in the same way. It is our power source. We are blessed with anger because it keeps us alive. Anger's default role is that it sends signals to all parts of our body to help us fight or flee. It gives us an instant boost of energy to perform an action. There was a time when our ancestors roamed the earth wearing goat skin and leaves. At that time, they were threatened by animals, or worse, ferocious beasts that waited for the chance to eat them. And of course, for survival tips, there was no internet at that time. To fight those beasts off, they needed fuel within. Anger filled the gap. Anger helped them defend themselves.

These days, there are even more devilish, vile and ferocious human beings out there. Human beings who want to suck the lives out of you. Can we counter them without using anger? Nope.

Anger is just a response to physical or mental pain. Hence it can be used in productive or counter-productive ways. And not to forget, it is just like electricity. It can power things up or electrocute you.

The answer lies in the fact that it is futile to relieve your anger, but it may turn out to be really productive to live your anger. Now how do you do it? Here are some points on anger repository's filling in and emptying out:

Remember: The people. You know how they told everyone you can never do anything in your life. You know how they laughed when you hinted to them about your dreams. Remember their faces, what they said, their laughter and their sarcasm. Prepare your anger repository by putting the first layer as your memory of them pointing at you.

Listen: To everything they said; just to ensure that you have a hold of the things that made you angry. When you are doing something that you know will help you hold your head high for the rest of your life, and if you need motivation, recall their faces and words. Tell yourself that if you did not spit on their faces by your achievements, your life is condemned to damnation.

Frustration: Anger and frustration are a unit. They go hand-in-hand. When things don't go as you desire, you are bound to get frustrated. That is directly proportional to anger. Put it into the repository and divert it into the course of your work so that you find a way to fly above your obstacles. The most famous line about this concept was spoken by Thomas Elva Edison. Everyone has heard of this: When questioned about his failed attempts to make the household light bulbs, he said, 'I have not failed 700 times. I have not failed once. I have succeeded in proving that those 700 ways will not work. When I eliminated the ways that will not work, I found the way that worked'. It was a clever way to put it in words. But his point was that his frustration led to positivity, in finding what he ultimately wanted. And today, the world bows to his greatness.

Hold on to that feeling: The most important rule. Do not spill your anger everywhere. There are very less chances that it will lead you anywhere unless you shoot a lucky shot. But a champion doesn't rely wholly on luck, does he? Angry? Want to take revenge? Somewhere inside, all of us love revenge. It depends on you, to decide how to take it. Do you want to do low, gentle damage to your enemy and leave him so that he comes back on you with a vicious blow? Or do you want to leave a devastating shot? If you choose the latter, showing all your fury at one time will not help you. Remember that a wounded snake is the one that is most dangerous. Remember that with you storing your anger you can kill that snake with one fatal blow. Remember to store your anger.

The point is that if a sentiment, however valid it maybe in its intent, doesn't inspire you to take action, it has no value to you. But if the intent of a particular sentiment isn't good, but you can use it, do that. I'm not a fan of ineffectual negativity, either. If it keeps you warm, fine. Keep it. But in my experience, most people in our lives who complain about everything aren't contributing either. So remember this throughout your life: Your anger is a gift and your frustration is a blessing.

A while ago, I read about a study titled *The art of Anger* in a psychology journal. Participants were shown objects they associated with a prize. Some, though, were first exposed to angry faces. Those shown the angry faces were more likely to want objects that they were subsequently exposed to. They showed more positive vibes and more *directed* aggression towards getting the prize, rather than letting the others. It is not about turning anger into positive energy. Anger *is* a positive energy. It is about applying or using it. It is a powerful motivating force. Believe me, when we see something that is great for us, we want it more when we're angry. Be it anything: a luxury item, good grades, or even that hot girl next door.

Just remember, though anger is dubbed as a vice and is used to charge you up towards achieving your goal, same is not true for fear. For motivation, people try to instill into their brains the fear of complete failure. They think it is an effective method of motivation. But fear is something else. Fear is enough to make you passable in whatever it is you're afraid of being or not being. Fear can never be a motivator. But anger is, and it is a strong one.

When you are chased by a lion, you stop running when the lion goes away, or you die. That is just survival. To be successful, you need to be the lion. The lion is always running. The lion is always fearless. The lion is always angry. Be hungry, be angry, and chase everything and everyone down until they give up or until you outrun them. Relish in your triumph, but move on to the next thing because you're still hungry and still angry.

Emotional intelligence theory divides 'aggressive feelings' into two parts: primary and secondary feelings. The primary feeling is the feeling we get just before getting angry. That is, just before the heat starts to rise. Secondary feeling is anger itself. The key is to remember during the course of primary feelings that you have to pass *through* the secondary feeling and store it. And BAM. You will win.

You must allow yourself to feel anger, and let it grow on you to the point where you feel you can control it. Anger isn't to be ignored and thrown. It is to be respected and heard. It acts as a guide, letting us know when we've taken a wrong turn in life, or if we need to try a different path. Think of anger as a compass, a compass that will point you to the right direction and the right place.

The trick is to funnel your anger into worthwhile pursuits and not letting that anger get the best of you. Anger is more useful in that it can push you past mental barriers that would normally limit you. It is the greatest motivator to overcome anything in life.

But we have to remember this: though anger is a powerful motivator, it's also a double-edged sword. If you use too much anger, you can accomplish a goal, but also end up destroying or hurting someone or something else. Use too little, and you might not accomplish much. Aristotle once remarked, 'Anyone can become angry. That is easy. But to be angry with the right person, to the right degree, at the right time, for the right purpose and in the right way - that is not easy.'

Righteous anger is what that makes the difference. This is when you know what you are angry about, why you are making yourself angry, and are doing it with a clear, level-headed, positive intent. Anger contributes to motivation when it comes to competition and the attainment of something. The angrier a person becomes fighting for his life, the stronger he becomes. And there goes the trick behind all the wars won in history.

Don't you feel fierce and motivated when your goal is blocked? Home, college, work, anywhere? When an enemy locks you in dire straits, don't you get that feeling to tear him apart? Since anger is that strong force against your obstacles, it will tell you that can crush your foe. Not only that, it will help you in doing so. Now let us do an exercise. No, don't take trouble looking for a pencil or paper or anything. You can do this mentally.

1. Think of that one thing which makes you lose your temper the most.
2. Think of why it makes you angry.
3. When you find the answer to why, think of your first reaction to that why.
4. This reaction is associated with primary feelings. A primary feeling is something you feel just before you reach that stage where you are filthy angry.
5. Finally, think of the transition from primary to secondary feelings. A secondary feeling is good old true anger.

That is the transition where you have to remember that there is no need to express your secondary feelings. You can show it later, fiercely and with impact. Else it will be hollow and most of the time, destructive.

Now that we have talked about this motivator, let us move on to another and an equally important one.

Many *grown-ups* love WWE. But their love for WWE is pretty different. They aren't like those immature kids, crazy about a fake show on television. They are well aware of the choreographed moves, scripted storylines, and the infamous 'kayfabe' thing. And yet, they have an affinity for this meant-for-men-soap-opera.

They love it probably because of the dramatic storylines, girls in lingerie, bikes, dialogues and all that. But above all these, they subconsciously like the show because the wrestlers in the show display a great deal of endurance. They withstand physical pain. Falling and getting their ass kicked are some of the less torturous things they go through. Still, they never let anything overshadow their acting.

This is something nice, if not great. It means that humans know the value of withstanding pain. They know its importance. Just like anger, pain is something that champions utilize to reach their destination. If anger is the feeling that keeps us alive, pain is that feeling which does the same on a different level.

It is said that a man makes his self all by himself. But that isn't entirely true. A man cannot make himself and his life without suffering, for he is both the marble and the sculptor. Others may laugh at the pain he is enduring, but he knows how to shut them up. That is the true nature of pain. It makes people.

Theodore Roosevelt, the 26th President of the United States was very unlike the soft-toy that took his name (Read, *Teddy* Bear). He was one of the strongest guys the world knew, and he knew the value of pain. In his famous *Citizenship in a Republic* speech, he talked about 'The man in the arena':

It is not the critic who counts, not the man who points out how the strong man stumbles, or where the doer of deeds could have done them better. The credit belongs to the man who is actually in the arena, whose face is marred by dust and sweat and blood; who strives valiantly; who errs, who comes short again and again, because there is no effort without error and shortcoming; but who does actually strive to do the deeds; who knows great enthusiasms, the great devotions; who spends himself in a worthy cause; who at the best knows in the end the triumph of high achievement, and who at the worst, if he fails, at least fails while daring greatly, so that his place shall never be with those cold and timid souls who neither know victory nor defeat.

Mr. Roosevelt knew the true meaning of dust, sweat and blood. He has put that neatly into words here. When we define pain, it is just physical or mental suffering. But experiencing it is on a pretty different level. And that is far from defining it. People cannot define their own pain. Or what they're going through. But they can express it. Maybe seek some attention so that people come and console them about things that happened. But champions are different.

Champions know how to express pain, but they don't want to. Because they know only cowards and nincompoops want attention. Instead of this, just like anger, they use pain as some sort of alarm that pulls them up whenever they fall down.

Imagine you are a sleepy person, left in a jungle. You have to stay awake all night to save yourself from the wild. What do you do? The best answer would be to prick yourself all night with something sharp so that the irritation keeps you going through the night. That is close to what pain does. It keeps you alive.

There are times in life when you need a push, like a wave that takes you to the shore. Pain does just that. It ignites the fire inside you and tempts you to win. Due to generalized concepts our mind has made, we are forced to think that pain pulls us down. But strangely, it pushes us up ahead. And it does that by being a silent companion who is apparently a villain in the story but was helping us all along. And that is how the greatest stories are written, right?

Getting into some neuro-scientific stuff, when it comes to the neuroscience of pain, it is treated unlike other stimuli from the very outset. The intensity of pain is also relative to other stimuli around the area of pain. Turns out some pain pathways are gated by cells which receive input from pressure sensors. So pain is not just a signal, it's a very specific signal.

The neuro-scientific interpretation of pain splits it into four parts:

1. Awareness of the pain.
2. The sensation.
3. The emotional response.
4. Localization.

Each of these is handled by a different area of the brain, with sensation handled by something called the anterior cingulate gyrus and emotional response by the amygdala. This applies to all kinds of pain. Phew, that was heavy.

The point is now we know that there are specific parts for the reception of pain in our body. This means that pain is not just a sensation, but it is a necessity for a body. It is not a feeling to be ignored or suffered. It is something to be used and utilized.

This chapter is not asking you to be a masochist. The sane ones do not get entertained by *useless* pain. But when your path to become a champion sends down some heavy pain to deal with, you have to say 'Bring it on!' to it. Face it. There is no point running away. Running away will only help pain chase you down.

It was Shakespeare in *Romeo and Juliet*, who said, 'Parting is such a sweet sorrow.' Great oxymoron there, Shakespeare. But is *sweet sorrow* truly an oxymoron? Nope. Sorrow can be sweet. Pain can be sweet. You just need to use it wisely. Pain is good as it drives you towards where you want to be or what you want to be.

It is obvious that the pain we are talking about here is not limited to physical or emotional pain. It can be any, and the area of application of the use of pain can be any. There are no limitations in using pain.

Pain will:

Lift you up: You will be knocked down. Every time. But pain will push you up and help you stand on your legs to fight again. The very places and points where you felt pain will be fatal for your opponents.

Fuel you up: You will lose energy. You will feel empty. At this time, pain will give you some sudden shots of energy to fight with. It will fill you with power that you never knew you had.

Knock them down: Your instant reactions will confuse every obstacle you have and your endurance will generate great fear in the hearts of your enemies. When your enemies will see you withstanding pain, they will run away in fear.

Eliminate your fright: Whenever you will be under the influence of pain, you will learn to conquer your fears. In this process, pain will help uprooting all the dread you ever had.

Here is a small story a guy shared on an internet forum (rephrased).

I used to be an athlete in my teen years, playing soccer, basketball almost daily, was best at sprinting in school but then my life changed and I stopped exercising for around five years. I took up strength training and was bicycling. After a year, I broke my elbow (radial head was in four pieces) while mountain biking. I had two screws and was out of exercise for seven weeks. I decided to start running. It was my first time in over six years. The first time around, I had sharp pain in the lower back and had to stop at around five kilometres. I felt sad, but pumped myself up, to better myself.

Second time around I made it to five kilometres, and again couldn't go on. But as soon as I stopped, I was attacked by fierce, angry bugs. In about 30 seconds I was stung many times all over my body, ankles, quads, arms, fingers, face. There has been a lot of rain in Europe and the small park I was in was filled with bugs.

It was painful, very painful, I panicked, my eyes were filled with tears and I felt like I needed to run for my life. I ran as fast as I could, straight back home, which was about 7 kilometres away. Pain was the biggest motivator. I mean, what was I to do? I had a goal, I was focused, I was sober and rational about it, and ignored my physical limitations. In my head, I saw myself succeed; I created a picture of me running without limitations about my accomplishments.

I was stung 28 times. But the feeling I had was awesome. I understood that no one has physical limitations. I understood that without pain, no one can achieve anything in life, even if it is something trivial to get.

Withstanding pain makes you a true badass. There is nothing you can't deal with when you can withstand pain. The pain that makes people think will make you fall on your knees will actually make you rise when you use the pain to stimulate your desires. Anger and pain are blood brothers. They work the same way, yet with entirely different processes. They are meant to destroy you, but when worked upon, they both work wonders.

A winner goes slow and steady towards his goal. But a champion doesn't actually go slowly. A champion uses that catalyst to breathe life into him. That lightning bolt which finally shocks him into snapping out the rut he has been in, and finally pushes him over the edge.

You hold onto that power. It is just that one simple word, pain. You see, you already have the catalyst. It's just a matter of being honest with yourself. Go past the insecurity. Go past the little voice that says that doing that thing will hurt you. Instead let the pain flow through you, and just hold on. At that very point, you will find yourself invincible. You will find that you are accomplishing everything you craved for.

Friedrich Nietzsche had a great view on pain. According to him, pain compels people to descend to their ultimate depths, and makes them profound. Pain helps people interact better with themselves and understand their existence. Pain is not to be embraced, it is to be conquered. And that just requires a stable mind. Not stiff but flexible, yet stable mind.

Pain is often used with the word pleasure. A major part of human behavior deals with the need to gain pleasure and avoid pain. According to many, pleasure is a strong motivator. But which is the stronger amongst the two?

Now try to answer something else. Why is pleasure positive and pain negative? Pain is prima facie undesirable and pleasure is likewise desirable. It isn't possible to extricate the negativity or positivity from the sensations of pain or pleasure. Now, we are wired so that we feel pain in certain types of situations and pleasure in other, distinctive ones.

The situations where we feel pain are simply to give us a push towards our goals. There is no negativity in pain; it is just tricky to understand. But when you do understand the meaning of pain, you will find that you have discovered something that will take you to the very end of the path. You will find that something that was apparently meant to mislead you was the one thing helping you all along. You must have had a lot in your life. At some point, pain must have wrecked you emotionally, financially, physically, spiritually, mentally et al. This means that you now have an arsenal of weapons to help you get anything you want.

Attaching the painful experiences of the past to your current goals will give you that force you always needed. Let us do another mental exercise.

1. Think about a goal in your life.
2. Think about a painful experience you went through and want to avoid in the future. It is crucial that your goal and painful memory are somewhat related.
3. Link the goal and the experience.

4. Tell yourself that not achieving the goal will result in the pain you wish to avoid. Repeat.

You will find yourself closer to that goal now. Humans have a tendency to avoid pain. But you have to stop fighting against the human instincts and mold them to work for you. It is useless to try to throw away anger. It is useless to run away from pain. They both are made for use. They are made to strengthen you. Anger and pain are among the most useful and effective weapons you have at your disposal. You can use them at any time. And the better you are at using them, the easier it will be for you to dust off and march towards victory. Pain and anger drive human behavior and motivation and your success in life is based on the associations you have linked up in your brain. It's when you learn to use your pain and anger to your advantage, that you'll unlock your true potential.

Congratulations! You have conquered two great things. Remember, there is no better feeling in the world than to rip the heart from your enemy with rage and let it bleed on the battlefield. You are above your strengths, your weaknesses. You are above your pain. You are above every enemy and every single frenemy you know.

Keep reading, champion.

Respect and Belief

This decade has popularized a great term. 'Winning'. Winning at life, winning the internet, FTW. There are many winners around. Look around you, there will be many. There are many professionals, leaders, all of them. But champions?

There are distinct differences between winners and champions. Winners are good people who follow the regular set of rules to win. They adjust among people and go with the flow to win. They know that they have to just be on the track to win. Who are the champions then?

Champions do not look for rules to win and waste their time. Champions don't adjust; they make their way. Champions don't go with the flow; they flow. Champions don't stay on the track, they fly above others. Why do they do this? To win? No. A win is low pay for so much labor. They do this for one thing: respect.

Ask people what they want and a majority of them will choose money or power. When we break down these 'simple' words, we'll find interesting results.

Money: The root of all evil? Nope. It is actually the root of all causes for many. People breathe and die for money. And that's pretty good; at least they have a goal in their lives. But hold on, is that really a goal? Why do people want money? To buy themselves luxury, great clothes, what-not. And why do they do that? To show the high standards in their way of living. And why do they want to show high standards to people? Hold on.

Power: Power is a damn fine thing. The feeling of sitting high up than others and crushing people who disobey you, that is just great. Most of us want power. Extreme power, because it is something that you can use anywhere. Hold on, again, why do you want power?

Yes. Both ways lead to one destination: respect. You want money so that people respect you and the same for power. For some, money leads to power. But ultimately, everything leads to the one word which champions love: respect.

There are no 'forms' of respect. There is no universal definition of respect. If philosophers talk about respect, rappers rap on the very same topic. One has his own parameter for respect, but it goes on a whole new level for champions. Why is respect something we need to care about in the course of our journey when it will already be waiting for us when we will reach the end? This is because respect is that source of power which lights our path throughout our journey. It will help us at times everything else will fail. Moreover, it is a necessity rather than a want.

A champion has his own goals, but with them he looks for respect. Respect for himself and everything he has done. Respect is that prize which isn't just complimentary with the prize he wanted, but is necessary. You don't really need much explanation as to why to seek respect. You know that it is important. We just need to have a general idea of respect.

When it comes to respect, one must remember these things:

Name: Not the one you were given in your naming ceremony by your elders. But the one you are going to make. You will decide whether your name will be called respectfully or in a dull tone. You have to respect, and make people respect your name. How? Start by putting an end to do things anonymously. It is a small thing to do, but very effective. Whatever you do, make sure no one else claims your work and you don't do it anonymously except when it comes to charity. The point is to take responsibility for everything you do, and putting your name to everything you do. They say it takes years to make a name, but seconds to destroy one. But when you have that level of respect from people, no one can destroy your name in millennia to come. Think of Archimedes, Newton, Alexander the Great and Plato. If the seconds to destroy theory worked, their names would not have been here mentioned as examples in this book about champions. Doing things anonymously is not just cowardice, it is also shameful. Maintain the respect level by using your name. Associate your name with respectable things. Be a man of honor.

Ten Commandments of Respect: Remember them through thick and thin:

1. Don't be a pussy: Rule numero uno. Do not get scared by petty challenges. Remember that challenges are thrown to you just to check how tough you are. Stay strong, face whatever you are given and even spit on your challenge. Just do not act like a pussy.
2. Do not back down, stand up and fight: Never step even an inch back. If someone, or life throws you down something prepare yourself to fight against it.
3. Do what you say you will: Never become an empty utensil. Stay on your words, and fulfill what you promise.
4. No matter what happens, remember that you have to gather your strength to strike back: Many things can be summed up by using these two words that people from this decade love: *shit happens*. But then what you have to do is gather everything you have, all the courage, all the strength and put that against the odds.
5. Don't agree with people just to make them like you. Let them know you disagree in a polite and gentlemanly manner. Don't go like, 'Yes man, you are always right!' Never agree to any kind of bullshit. When you keep agreeing to someone's wrongdoings you may become that person's favorite for a while, but you will slowly lose all the respect. You can

afford to lose that person but never afford to lose respect.

6. Always strive to improve yourself physically and mentally: At any point of life if you find that you are not matching or if you are not one step ahead of the world around you; stop right there. Improve your skills, and then run. You will find yourself leading the way.
7. Be a worker: Do not be reluctant to work. No one is telling you to become a workaholic but you have to do your necessary work. Be an efficient worker.
8. Under-promise, over-deliver: Simply put, do not boast. Perform. Remember that people will heed to what you do rather than who you are. Under promise and over deliver.
9. Keep your promises: Never promise something you cannot deliver. But if you promise something, remember to fulfill that.
10. Admit when you are wrong: You will make mistakes on your way to become a champion. Acknowledge them. Acknowledging will help you work on them and improve on the parts where you are going wrong. If there is no need of admitting your mistakes publicly admit it to yourself. Instead of going crazy on yourself and blaming yourself blindly, acknowledge and improve.

Reflect: Reflect yourself in everything you do, everywhere you go, and everyone you meet. Champions are not impersonations of something or someone. They do not copy others and don't desire things they have. People go crazy about what others do and try to copy them. Be original, be yourself. Trying to be someone else is pretty much the most disgusting thing in the world. Reflecting yourself doesn't mean that you do some different things to be a hipster, it means that you make a proper persona and an identity of yourself so that when people are reminded of you they have a respectable and distinct mental image of you. Be real and carry your distinct persona.

Earn: Asking for respect is for suckers. Earning respect is a different thing. It requires devotion, pledging to everything you do, and your entire body resonating with the brain. When you put in everything to do something, you are bound to get respect.

Differentiate: Fear and respect are way, way apart. They are on opposite poles. You cannot try to instill fear in people just so they respect you. That would be ridiculous because it isn't respect. Most people forget the differences between fear and respect. But a champion knows that if he has to win over his people, he cannot do that with them standing afar from him. For a champion it is a great achievement to instill fear in his enemy's heart, but fear in his allies' heart is a different notion. A champion's allies respect him instead of running away from him.

Let me illustrate the meaning of true respect in another way. You must have attended many events in school or college. You may have coordinated and organized some. You know that there are two types of people divided when an event is organized. One is the staff and organizers, the other is the audience. Wait, there is a third kind. The third kind is the one in whose honor the event is organized. That person is the reason behind the event. Yes, the audience gets respect. Organizers get more respect. But true respect is given to the person who is the reason for that event. Be that person. Be the person who gets ultimate respect.

Respect is simply a crown for the champions. You may be rich, you may be contented with life, you may be happy, but if you have no respect, everything mentioned is pointless. If we do not get into the theories, respect can be broadly divided into self-respect and respect given and received.

Self-respect is something that you must have read about in school in one of your moral values classes. Obviously the foundation of instilling self-respect in yourself must have been weak because in those classes it was often confused with doing good things to others, doing well to nature and so on. But self-respect is doing good to *yourself* before doing nice things for anyone or anything else. It is keeping yourself up in your eyes.

You know what? No one else must really matter to you. If you have to go against the world for your respect, go ahead and do it. It is impossible that you will not succeed in that condition. With self-respect comes everything you want to get to the place you want to. It is like that good old Swiss Army Knife.

Respect is to be given and received. Pick any person on earth and you will find that if you want to make him work up to his abilities, fear will not help. Neither will greed. It will be respect. Respect works like grease when your cogwheels are jammed. Because it is the ultimate aim of anything you are doing or you want to do.

Respect is surely a great motivator. But what about the time when you completely lose it? Can self-respect and the respect given by the people be regained?

Yes.

And that time will surely come, when you will walk on the street just losing at life. You will find people virtually throwing stones at you, laughing at you like you are some sort of jester, and saying things about you. What you have to do is to put your hood back on and keep walking. And under that hood, think of your next plan, about what can you do to regain respect.

The great Birbal once said, 'Respect lost by a drop cannot be regained by filling tanks.' He was right, but many misunderstood him. It may not be regained by filling tanks, but it sure as hell can be regained by mending things you have done and building up on them. Respect *can* be regained. It stands true for self-respect as well. For this, let us refer to a famous story found on the internet about some guy called Sparky.

He was called Sparky after a comic-strip horse named Spark Plug. Sparky was, well, weird. He hated school unlike other children hated school. He hated school because he never understood anything that was taught to him. No, he wasn't dyslexic and stuff. He just never got what they tried to explain to him in school. He failed in every subject in the eighth grade. He flunked physics in high school, earning zero. He also flunked Latin, Algebra and English. And his record in sports wasn't any better. Though he did manage to make the school's golf team, he promptly lost the only important match of the season. Oh, there was a consolation match; he lost that too.

And this went on through his youth, Sparky was awkward socially. No one really cared about him all that much. In fact, Sparky was astonished if a classmate ever said hello to him outside of school hours. There's no way to tell how he might have done at dating. He never once asked a girl out in high school. He was too afraid of being turned down, or perhaps laughed at. Sparky was a loser. He, his classmates, heck, everyone knew it. Yes, he lost all respect and self-respect.

One thing was important to Sparky, however. Drawing. Though he had no respect for himself, he was proud of his artwork. No one else appreciated it. But that didn't seem to matter to him. He 'put that hood on and kept walking.' In his senior year of high school, he submitted some cartoons to the yearbook. The editors rejected the concept. Despite this brush-off, Sparky was convinced of his ability. He even decided to become an artist. He put the hood on again.

So, after completing high school, Sparky wrote to Walt Disney Studios. They asked for samples of his artwork. Despite careful preparation, it too was rejected. One more confirmation that he was a loser. And yeah, another time to put the hood on.

Sparky didn't give up, still. Instead, he decided to tell his own life's story in cartoons. The main character would be a little boy who symbolized the perpetual loser and chronic underachiever. You know him well. Because Sparky's cartoon character went on to become a cultural phenomenon of sorts. People readily identified with this 'lovable loser.' He reminded people of the painful and embarrassing moments from their own past, of their pain and their shared humanity.

The character soon became famous worldwide. It became a legend. Charlie Brown.

And Sparky, the boy whose many failures never kept him from trying, whose work was rejected again and again, is the highly successful cartoonist Charles Schultz. His cartoon strip, 'Peanuts' continues to inspire books, T-shirts and Christmas specials.

The toughest part is that there is no literal cheat-sheet for respect. You cannot just think about getting respect, follow the method and get back what you have lost. You have to work for it, make a name for yourself, and then in the process you will find that you have gained immense respect. In other words, put the hood back on when you lose respect, keep planning and keep working. Then, strike back to earn your respect.

Do not confuse the word honor with the word respect. People keep interchanging the words when it comes to their usage, and that is where they go wrong. The definition for respect goes like this: Respect is when we provide an ethical value to the person in such a degree that they are highly esteemed in terms of personal perspective. Honor is more an assessment of a person's social status and degree. People even rate honor above respect. That is arguable. But there is a line which is unarguably correct: A champion may dishonor his enemy, but he will never disrespect. Dishonoring your enemy is acceptable when your enemy has broken you apart. To dishonor him, is to win a small war over him. But disrespecting? That means you are underrating your enemy, and that will make your enemy fiercer. That will make him strike with more strength.

Speaking about respect, what is its relation to success?

We have all been brainwashed by the media, by our peers, by our parents, by our mentors, teachers, to achieve this thing called success. For them success is getting admission in a big college, getting good grades and a big pay. But the thing is, no one can ever define success for you.

You can look up the definition of success in the dictionary or on the internet, but that would do a large injustice to you. Success is really a random word. What are words, they are meanings of associations. They are just ideas that we learn to attach to a concept. The word success cannot be universally defined.

Don't get deluded and confused by different conceptions of success. Let us talk about this: what is success, in general? Success is the magnitude of the footprint that you leave on society. It is about how many people you had an effect on and what type of an impact you had. Success is the respect you get from people. Success is proportional to respect. When you are after success, you are after respect.

Now that we have started talking about it, how to be 'after success'? For that, here's another great theory with a silly name. It is called the Muffin Recipe Theory.

If you are handed a muffin recipe and you follow it and the muffin turns out ugly and disgusting, does it say anything about you? No, of course not, it was a bad recipe. Now, let's say you are overweight. Is this because there is something wrong with you or because your recipe to be healthy is bad?

This applies to everything. Success is a measure of the quality of the recipes you use, and is not a measure of you. The point is that you actually never fail. You just learn that your process won't produce the result you want. All you need to complete your work is a good recipe. You need to 'know' about things.

There are three ways to get recipes:

1. The first way is to borrow the recipe from somebody else. For this, use role models and study success stories. You want to be an entrepreneur, look up what successful entrepreneurs do and follow them. But that will not be *your* recipe. It will be someone else's. It will be apt for their definition of success.
2. The second way is to try something on your own, get a wrong result, and then refine your approach. This is how most of life is, learning through trial and error.
3. The third way is a hybrid of the first and second one. You don't need to follow successful people here, you don't need to use trial and error. What you can do is to learn the mistakes of people who failed and try not to do that. This is the smartest way of getting a recipe: by not making the mistakes that the others did.

It would be wonderful if finding a new recipe for anything in life was as easy as finding a new muffin recipe. You will start baking a lot of muffins, many ugly and disgusting. Maybe then you will take examples from ugly muffins others are making, until you start making your own delicious ones. The point is to discover your own recipe to make your own muffins. The point is that you are doing things to gain respect. All to find your own success.

Many people spend their entire lives working to intimidate people by their power. That is fear and not respect. People's fear may make you satisfied and happy but in the long run you can be assured that the same people will uproot you as an authority and will interfere with your power as well. But getting respect is something else. The respect you get will be with you till eternity. Hold your respect high above everything. Chisel yourself in a way that no one disrespects you. Stand up to people who make fun of you. Stand up to bullies. Stand up to everyone who poses as a threat to your respect. Champions value respect. They value it above anything else.

There is no need of trying hard to get respect. Because when you will start trying hard and seeking respect, you will turn into an arrogant douche bag. How? Well when you will start trying hard to get respect, you will start boasting and exaggerating about your tiny achievements in order to get appreciation. People will only dislike you if you start doing that, not appreciate you.

Instead of trying hard, what you should do, is to keep running on your path keeping your head up and remembering your duties. What you should do is to be who you really are, and not throw your persona away.

Now, there is something else we must talk about. Something different. Answer this: What do you think of yourself right now?

If someone hands you something, do you believe that you will never let it fall? If you are given an opportunity to soar, do you believe that you will make the most of it? If you are caged in a room with no doors and windows, do you believe that you can break those walls around you and escape? Well, do you?

Here enters belief. The very basis of your existence.

Cogito ergo sum; I think, therefore I am. René Descartes was a sheer genius in quoting this line. Belief can shake the world, be it in any form.

There is a great misconception about belief. People often relate this word to being follower of some religion. But the belief we are talking about isn't the same thing. We are talking about a general idea of belief. Your beliefs may include a religion, an ideology, a person, a thing or anything else. Your belief may include yourself. And that is something to be highlighted. Believing in yourself is more important than believing in other things.

According to the famous author Sam Harris, beliefs are an acceptance of a certain statement as representing the actual state of the universe (or something else). This is a complicated, but a nice way to understand the term belief. We believe about the state of a particular thing. Another reasonable take on belief is by Robert Brandom. According to him, beliefs are commitments. They are things you take responsibility for, in particular a justificatory task responsibility. When the context is appropriate, you are responsible for justifying your commitments.

Now that we understand the concept of believing, we must understand why belief is necessary for champions. Not only this: we have to understand why champions have to choose their beliefs and make amendments at some points in life.

The simplest answer is: One must choose their beliefs because the reality they perceive is not static. As new information comes in, one must reevaluate how they understand the world. Think of all the beliefs children have, which they perceive as facts, and how these transmute as they get older and learn more. If we were born with beliefs, or if they were ascribed to us, we would be rigid in our mindsets and inflexible in a changing world. In nature, creatures must be adaptable, and it is in large part humans' adaptability that allowed survival.

From another route, consider the brain on a physical level. New connections are made by the brain itself as it takes in new information. Babies start relatively blankly and their brains begin to exhibit intelligence. If beliefs are interpreted as a series of connections in the brain, they must have been made by the brain itself, and as such are subject to change as much as any other thought or pathway. There goes the anatomy of belief. Now comes the major part. 'Believing in yourself.' People attend lectures about it, read books about it, ask people about it, but most of them have a hard time understanding it.

Is this line coherent: 'Believing in yourself'? How does one do this? How does one put this into practice? For this, I have a simple exercise for all of you.

Live one day as a person you want to be.

Actor? Philosopher? Sportsperson? The greatest guy in the world? Well, mould your body for a day just to be the person you want to be. Do your regular stuff. Go to work. Do whatever you do every day, but just remember to be what you want to be.

What is the point? Well, as soon as you know who you want to be and you already know that - you are that person in the future. You will start believing in yourself, and work for that dream. Yes. This exercise promotes daydreaming, so do it! It will surely fire you up, and you will start believing in yourself and your goals.

Daydream for just one day in your life. Yes, prolonged daydreaming is lethal, but one-day-daydreaming is amazing. After that, if you really, really want to fill in the confidence and belief meter inside you every day, do this little exercise: daydream inside your bathroom. Whenever you are bathing, think of the interviews you will have. Think of the stories you will tell, think about how you conquered all odds and became what you were destined to be. Do that till you reach for your towel.

This isn't senseless or weird. This is just to fill the bar of belief meter inside you. This will help you believe in yourself more and make you work.

A part of your rational brain must be in doubt about what is written above. Hell, your entire brain might be sounding alarm bells. Let us try to make this text and the concept of dream big clearer.

The 'dream' thing is a bit weird. Many people around us preach saying, 'follow your dreams' and the other side keeps saying, 'Be a rationalist. Do your work.' It is damn confusing. Which side we should listen to, now? It is true that a lot of people dream, while only a few make it to the top. What is the difference between dreamers and non-dreamers? Where should we go? Should we dream or work?

Dreaming big and working hard is definitely not a dichotomy. Working hard achieves things. But hard work without a dream is a day job, not a masterpiece. Dream and work for your dreams. What you should do is, not spend all your time dreaming. Dreams don't come true by themselves. The text written before this holds true every time. Dream of who you want to be, believe in the dream and it will put your ass to work and make you emerge a champion.

Sometimes, you may think that you do not have that factor that will make you speed up to your goals, that you don't have those talents, those traits. Here is something: There are around 7–7.5 billion people in the world. And there are a billion things, talents and good traits to have. When someone is born, nature does some mathematics, permutations and combinations, and gives you a specific set of skills. Every set is unique. No one in the world owns the set you have, no one. You have to discover those skills and complete your set. How? Believe.

I am not trying to instill a sense of over-confidence in you. I am just asking you to take a peek into yourself and find that gem that will make you shine amongst the seven billion people in this world. Most of them never do that and grow old thinking that they never had that factor in them. Oh screw that factor! You always did have it in you! You were just too lazy to find it. You were too skeptical to believe in yourself.

People reach the age of 70, look back and realize that they did not accomplish much in their lives. It is simply because they had their fair share of chances to believe in what they saw they could do, but they did not believe. Some even realize the chances they had to believe in themselves, but then they think it is too late. There are many bad feelings in this world, but the worst feeling is looking back and realizing that you had the power to rule the world you were in, but you were skeptical about yourself and did not use that power.

Being a thinker is great, but being skeptical about yourself totally sucks. You have to believe in yourself to do anything. You should put your thoughts on yourself and about your abilities but you shouldn't doubt on your power. The moment you start believing in yourself, it will be marked as the first step towards conquering the fort you want to conquer. The moment you make yourself realize that you can perform extraordinary feats will be the moment that will make you unstoppable.

Eventually, you will start believing in yourself. Eventually the day will come when you will sit down and will not regret anything you did because you will understand that your every move led you to the point you will be at, that day. Eventually you will understand the power of belief. But the thing is to understand it at the right time.

Second to believing in yourself is believing in the things you do. No, both phrases aren't the same. One may believe in himself but at the same time have doubts about what he is doing. Or one may believe in what he is doing but not believe in himself. A champion understands that believing in himself and believing in anything he does has to be in resonance and in harmony. He follows exactly that.

That said, a proper and logical aim is needed for a strong belief. You need to aim for the right thing. Do you know about moths? There are some species of moths which navigate using the sun. They constantly fly towards it in an attempt to reach it. It makes you wonder whether these moths died in peace knowing that they accomplished their goal in life. You may aim for something that is apparently near impossible for you but you must then justify it. To divide it into categories, there are three kinds of people in 21st Century:

1. The first are those who just enjoy reading Wikipedia. They love the gossip and stuff written about celebrities.
2. The second are those who want to make it to Wikipedia. They want to have an authentic article about themselves and their stories.
3. The third are those, who, along with making it to Wikipedia, want a 'legacy and influence' section added to their page.

If you are reading this, you are probably not the person that belongs to the first category. You may be the person who falls into the second category, or the third category.

Now if you are the third kind, and want to be a legend and a champion, then you have to be a believer. Belief isn't just important, it's a necessity here.

We have all had bad days in our life, days when we did not have anything to smile for, or to be positive about, days when everything was gloomy, sad and saturnine. Now think of that one day in the future, which will be the worst day of all. The worst day of your entire life. No, do not picture that day as a series of mishaps.

It's the day when you will wake up and realize that you have done nothing particularly significant or important in your life and it's way too late to change. At this point you'll be too old, too beaten up and tired to do anything about it. You will realize that you are simply like the other 99% of society and have wasted away a life, merely existing for the sake of it. All your dreams and ambitions left untouched and unexplored.

The day when you will look into the mirror, you will find yourself staring at a person who did not believe in himself and the things he did. You will find yourself looking at a person with lifeless eyes, and someone who is helpless.

But you know what? That day can be evaded. A champion never, ever faces such a day. A champion believes in himself and whatever he does from the very start. That worst day will never come in your life if you start believing in yourself from this very moment.

You may read this book all you want. You may read this anywhere you want, on a train, in an airplane, at home, in your hostel or anywhere else. You may read the book twice, thrice or even more. But the things written here will only work if you will believe in them.

Now we will talk about a strange word. This word will be discussed twice in this book in different chapters. Here is the first usage of this word: 'Faith'. For many, the word faith and belief are the same. But obviously they are not. They are interrelated, but they are not same. We need to learn the difference between both of them in brief. Faith refers to confidence in something. It doesn't necessarily require justification, because it is something that is generally accepted. Faith can be called as a form of belief. Belief, in a technical sense, is the attitude we take towards propositions we believe to be true. Is there any other way to believe in yourself? Yes, there is one. It is called controlled yet excessive self-confidence.

Keep telling yourself that you are a genius, and that you have everything in you that takes to conquer the world. Will that turn you into a self-loathing, over confident jerk? Yes. But then notice how the word control is added to excessive self-confidence. Define a limit to your self-confidence and keep filling yourself up with self praises till that limit is touched. That will help you getting a lot of belief in yourself.

Think of anyone you know who is more successful than you are. How are they so successful in their lives? How are they more successful than you? Do you lack some qualities or talents that they have that made them reach the position they are now? Nope.

The fact is that they don't have the qualities, or the set of talents you possess. In fact no one in the world has those talents. All you need is to acknowledge those talents, and believe in what you are.

Another thing is to stop telling yourself that others' opinions are important. This is a pretty common line that you will read in many books, but do this now, implement it. Some people think that unless everyone agrees with them, they are wrong. Honestly, how can you rely on people when it is a question about yourself and your journey? Be who you are and think what you want to think, that is it. To explain this, let us read a story.

Once, there were some (say, anthropomorphic) tiny frogs who gathered for a competition. The goal was to reach the top of a real high tower. A big crowd gathered around the building to see the race and cheer on the contestants.

The competition began. Honestly and pretty obviously, no one in the crowd believed the frogs would reach the top of the tower. Throughout the race, people shouted things like:

'To hell with them, it is damn difficult!'

'No one can make it to the top! I mean look at them!'

'They will all fall down. Veterinary doctor, anyone?'

'It is impossible!'

'Someone, tell them they are not Spiderman!'

'Are they insane?'

'They will surely collapse!'

They were somewhat right. The tiny frogs began collapsing, one by one, except for the ones who, in a fresh tempo, were climbing higher and higher.

The crowd continued, 'Stop it! It's too difficult!'

More tiny frogs heard them, got tired and gave up. But one stubborn jerk refused to give up. He kept on climbing. The crowd continued to berate and snicker at him. But he did not stop.

At the end of the race, all had given up climbing the tower except for that one tiny frog who was the only one who reached the top. Astounded, all of the other frogs wanted to know how this one frog managed to do it. They asked him how he had found the strength to succeed and reach the goal.

The champion frog did not respond. It turned out that he was deaf!

There is no moral of this story, there is only a point proven. The point is that if you keep hearing what people say, it will deviate you from your belief in yourself.

The main idea is to trust yourself and put your control in your own hands. You know that it is your body, your brain and your journey. You can trust only one person with these precious things and that is yourself. Give your strings, your remote control to yourself and see where that takes you. Giving control to yourself will never let you down.

Your belief will change your world. It will catapult you straight to the zenith. Think of it as a strange power that you possess. Unfortunately, many people ignore this power. They know that if they believe in getting something, that thing will be theirs. But they are too skeptical to believe. Be rational, not skeptical.

Who are you? A mere human? Nope. You are a force. You have been a force throughout your life. The thing is, you are a small force. A meek force, that is. All you need is to bring in belief in your life. Being a force, belief will make you stronger than ever.

Somewhere, deep in the quiet little recesses of your mind you are hearing a small voice that is rolling and growling. It will slowly grow into a cacophony until at last it becomes clear. Try to concentrate and listen to that voice. That voice isn't saying much, but just one word. 'Believe.'

Here is something posted by some anonymous guy on the online image board, 4chan:

I don't know you. I don't know a thing about you. I don't know where you come from, where you're going, or why you do what you do. I don't know if we'd get along if we met. But there is one thing that I do know: You are capable of much more than you have been led to believe.

As I am writing this, there are seven billion people walking and breathing on our humble rock. The overwhelming, vast majority of them will pass through their 720,000 hours like a match struck in the wind. Hardly noticed, scarcely remembered.

Tomorrow, as you go about your day, take you time to look around. Are there a lot of people around? What do you see? You see mediocrity. You see average. You see everything about yourself that you hate, that you fear, but that you have been conditioned to believe is acceptable. You want to do 'fine'.

I am here to tell you that you will NOT *settle for what is fine. You will* NOT *settle for a good job. Fine is for the losers. Fine is for the guy who skipped the last set of his workout because he just didn't feel like it. Fine is for the guy who cheated on his work because he just couldn't do it anymore. Fine is for the guy who took a nap instead of doing his job. Fine is for the guy who got the job, but not the one he wanted. That guy made second place. He has never embraced pain, personal sacrifice, or thrown himself into the fires of dedication. Most importantly, and starting today, this guy is* NOT YOU.

You are not this person. You are destined for greatness. You have it inside of you, and you know it. You have always known it, you have felt it as a faint thumping in your gut. It is clawing, scratching, struggling to be set free. It needs your help. As long as you hold yourself to the standard of 'average,' that is all you will ever be. In your dreams you aren't average, so why the hell are you settling for it now? What are you not doing right now? What is eating at the back of your skull? Go do IT.

*You know what it is, champion. The time to act is now. You will burn. You will suffer. Your demons will not be defeated easily. Every step of the way they will whisper in your ear that you aren't good enough. That you aren't meant to succeed. 'Just give up,' they will mutter, 'you'll never be the best.' '*NO*,' you will reply. You will embrace suffering. You will finish that last repetition. You will claw through the agonizing pain, you will destroy the mediocre pussy in your head, and you will break boundaries. You will rise above the rest. You will realize your potential.*

You, are no average man. Now go do what you were destined to do. End of story.

Keep reading, champion.

Hope and Anxiety

A lot has been written on this topic. Philosophers have discussed it for generations. Many movies have used this as a central plot. Infinite books are written on this topic itself. But let us think of this: Can hope really stay with us in dire straits?

It is said, 'We know in our bones that hope is everything, but in the back of our mind we suspect hope is nothing at all.' Yeah, we do know about this thing called hope. But at that point of life where you are being tested, you will probably forget this word. This is pretty normal as humans have a prolonged habit of abandoning hope. This habit we have is with us from a long time. Need proof? Heard of Pandora? Most of you must have, you can skip reading the story. For others, here it is:

In Greek mythology, there were two Gods named Epimetheus and Prometheus.

The Elder God, Zeus declared that humans did not deserve fire. Prometheus gave man the secret of fire even though Zeus had told all the gods not to do just that. Zeus was furious that his order had been ignored. As punishment, he chained Prometheus to a rock for many years.

Zeus wasn't satisfied. Once Prometheus was chained to a rock, Zeus went after his brother, Epimetheus. He did not chain Epimetheus to a rock. He had a more sneaky punishment in mind.

First, he ordered the handyman, the maker of things - Hephaestus - to make him a daughter. Hephaestus made a woman out of clay. He brought her to life, and then brought her to Zeus. Zeus named his beautiful new daughter Pandora.

Zeus knew that Epimetheus was lonely. He told him that his brother had to be punished and that's why he was chained to a rock. But he felt sorry that this punishment left him without the company of his brother. That's why he had decided to give Pandora in marriage to him.

Epimetheus was kind-hearted and gentle and thoughtful, but he was not dumbass. He knew that Zeus was up to something. But he loved Pandora at first sight.

Zeus gave the newlyweds a gift. Some books say it was a jar, some say it was a box. Whatever it was, it was locked. It came with a note which said, 'Do not open.' Attached to the note was a key.

You can guess what happened next. It was Pandora whose curiosity got the better of her. One day, she used the key to open the box. As she raised the lid, out flew all the bad things in the world today: Fear, sickness, sloth, et al. She hastened to close the container but she was late and the whole contents had escaped, except for one thing that lay at the bottom – Hope. And hope remained in the box forever.

In other variations of the story, hope escapes just when Pandora was about to close the lid. In either case, we can infer that hope is something we all have kept ignoring involuntarily since the inception of universe. There is no explanation as to why we do this, but yes; we keep running away from hope.

This is good in a way because it proves that we are mature. We are sane. We know that merely dreaming of things will not make us get them. We think that if we hope for something, that will keep us under a great illusion. An illusion we would not be able to break. That is true. Hope can drive a man crazy. It can even make him a paranoid schizophrenic, if the thing he hopes is fundamentally impractical.

But then the question to essentially deal with: Why hope?

We just talked about how we think that hope drives a man crazy. And believe it or not, that is what a champion needs: a pinch of craziness towards achieving his goals. A champion needs to be crazy to get his achievements, and contain that craziness in him. A champion's craziness is generally on the lines of 'controlled insanity'. This craziness keeps reminding the champion that he can do much more than what he thinks. He needs to know that even if he loses everything, he stands a great chance to rebuild everything. That is where hope enters into the game.

You will not find a single success story without a hint of hope in it. It has to be everywhere. We just do not give it the place it deserves.

If you cannot hope about what you want to achieve, and where you want to be, you will not achieve that. When you hope for something, the gears in your mind start working in that direction. You will think in the way you are meant to think.

Remember how we talked about the differences between faith and belief? The word faith will interfere in this chapter too. We need to understand the difference between faith and hope. Because we are often deluded and confuse the former with the latter. When I interact with people in an intellectual assembly, I often find them talking about the difference between hope and faith. I found out that there are many conflicting views on the topic. Some even consider them the same. But what about the general view?

Some points can be chalked out:

1. You can have faith without having hope, and that you can also have hope without having faith. They do not go hand-in-hand by default.
2. Faith usually means the acceptance of a truth-claim without sufficient justification. Hope is more of a feeling or wanting.
3. Hope is a preference, faith is an assertion.
4. Faith is reliance on someone. Hope is an expression of your personal strong desire.

Though these points do not give us the desired differences between the two, and they are complex, they do tell us the neutral characteristics. We may have faith on our present, but hoping for the future is something we need. We need to have two distinct, clear images of hope and faith in our brain. And understand that right now, we are not talking about acceptance; we are talking about the feelings.

Yes, there are *hipsters* who detest hope and believe that it detaches us from the reality. But they are just misinterpreting hope. They are talking about something called false hope. False hope is something that discourages people from seeking real solutions. They think they don't have to seek because they're promised a favorable outcome anyway. That is not what a champion wants to do. He doesn't just want to aim, he wants to hit it.

From putting a man on the moon to asking a girl out, hope can do anything for you. It will not be easy to hope for better days when you are neck deep in shit. But the point is, it will be worth it.

You just have to remember this four lettered word to get going. This word will always give you a strong push in situations where it becomes difficult to breath, or when it is all darkness around you.

Moreover you need to understand the value of hope and think of it as something more than a mere feeling. You need to tell yourself that all is not lost, and will never be. And now we shall discuss how to do that.

How to hold on to hope in dire straits?

Think of this. There is a huge mountain of a task you are supposed to do. You are at ground zero. You have nothing on you and you are standing naked right at the bottom. You have nothing, virtually. No personality, no idea how to use your brain to reach up, nothing. But there is a faint light right up there which is giving you a little warmth and radiance.

What do you do now? You look right up there, acknowledge the light and gather strength using that warmth to rise up, to climb up. That light is obviously hope.

The point made above is to *acknowledge* hope. That is the first step. When you know that in any situation you are in, however hard it is, you will always have that one tool called hope you can escape out of anywhere. Acknowledging hope makes you start paving your way towards removing the obstacle.

Now while you are climbing up, you may encounter some other small gaps, crevices and distractions. Now what? You look down and you will find that you have moved considerably farther than you started. You look up and find you goal closer. You also find that though the small obstacles are distracting you from acknowledging the light, you are constantly reminding yourself of it as you know it is the only aid you have to climb up.

Remember hope. The worst mistake people make is that they start doing something grabbing hope, and they slowly lose the grip of it themselves. Champions don't do that. They keep holding on till they finally reach their destination. Remember hope through thick and thin. Write it down, put a firm mental note in your brain, keep chanting it and do whatever you can to remember that you can always hope.

So we come down to just two things to hold on to hope in tough times:

1. Acknowledging: You know that hope is right within you. You know that hope is that supernatural thing which will light the fire in you to run and reach your goals. But there is something absurd about us: though we have the knowledge about hope, we do not acknowledge it. But it isn't our mistake. From our childhood, we are told stories about brave hearts and legends. We learn about their *qualities*. We quietly tell ourselves to become like them. As we grow up, reality hits, and BAM! We suddenly realize that such things sound good in books, and things are entirely different when it comes to reality. With this realization, we forget every value we have ever known and turn into a *normal* being. Among many of such values, hope is something that gets affected the most. As we grow up, we lose the grip of hope and let it go. Even after losing the grip, when it hides somewhere inside us, we ignore it. Hope calls us out every time we are in pain, but we suppress its voice. But now, start listening to the voice that says, 'Stop bullshitting, do your work and keep hoping.' There is one fact that can never go wrong and that is the day you start acknowledging hope, no one can destroy you, ever.
2. Remembering: When times are bad, your brain starts thinking about a lot of things. In this process, it blocks itself from your feelings. It just takes

several obstacles to divert you from heeding to your feelings. When this over-flow of the thinking fluid starts taking place, you start forgetting about hope. And you will forget hope in such a way that you will not even remember that there is an existence of a particular thing called hope. Life throws a champion down many things, but he cannot counter them without hope. So, just remember that hope will always be with you. Just remembering it in tough times will take you through.

You don't have to do anything special to hope. Just acknowledge and remember and you will find yourself facing that bright side that you are supposed to. Now let us add '-lessness' to the term we are talking about.

Hopelessness is something that doesn't leave us easily. For removing this obstacle we need to remember the small victories rule.

The steps to follow small victories rule are:

1. Set new, minute goals that are achievable.
2. The goals must be easily in reach and should start small chain of good things happening to you.
3. Give some time to those goals. In fact, give them priority for a while if you are really low on hope.
4. Accomplish them.

You will find some new vibrations inside you and your hope filled up again. If you set your eyes on small victories when you are hopeless, your wins will rejuvenate you and destroy the hopelessness. There will be a time when you will find yourself increasingly hating hope. On days where you will feel good, or you will feel like something positive is happening, things will suddenly seem to get significantly worse. You will feel like punching the people behind the 'Keep hoping' campaign. It will feel like any time it looks like getting better, it is just life looking to bring you up so it can knock you down. This is the time you need to grab tighter. This is the time when you need to suspend your disbelief about hope and there is nothing truer than this: you will be surely rewarded.

Hope is the only thing that will keep you going. All the other feelings will leave you. They will turn you into someone who is entirely empty; bereft of feelings. But hope will stay in your body just like it did in Pandora's Box.

Yes it is hard. It is damn hard to put in everything behind a feeling when you have don't have much. But that's what champions do, don't they? They go all in. Champions know that if they will hope for what they want to happen, no one on this planet can ever change that. They put all their trust in hope when things don't go their way, and later emerge out victorious.

There is one small factor people ignore: Make sure you know what you are hoping for. Even while hoping, our mind faces diversion. This diversion may elude you and you may start hoping for multiple things at ones, including things you don't even need. Just make sure what you are hoping for, and have a purpose.

One more thing to note about hope is that it is comparable to a rubber band or elastic, you can pick one.

The point is that it can be stretched. How can hope be stretched? Well it can be stretched to adapt to situations as they change. You can hope for good, better, the best and then the very best. The thing we are learning here is how high your hopes go depends upon the intensity of your desire. It is just like a role-playing game where each trait has its own perks. Low hopes do not carry risks, need lesser beliefs, but do not yield much. High hopes carry risk, need more belief, but the pay-off is amazing. Now it depends on how badass you are. You can hope as much as you want, but you have to believe in your hope.

Moving on, let us talk about something we all experience every other day. Anxiety is interpreted in the dictionary as a feeling of worry, nervousness, or unease about something with an uncertain outcome. Hope is a feeling about an uncertain outcome too, but Hope and Anxiety are on opposite poles. Anxiety is something you are bound to feel at some point in life. Fear of results: anxiety. Fear of losing something: anxiety. Fear of not accomplishing something: anxiety. Fear of not reaching where you want to: anxiety. It can be visibly noted that the word fear is predominantly highlighted pompously in this paragraph. But that is how it arrives in your brain: accompanying anxiety.

Anxiety sucks. It will drain you of your energy, power and strength. It provokes you to take bad decisions that ruin what you have made happen and possible. It will ask you to step down. It will tell you that being a champion is not great. The worst part is that it grows over you faster than anything else. You will just blink, let a thought enter your mind, and before you know it, that thought would have already turned to anxiety.

Champions have a lot to think about. They cannot have the place for anxiety in their lives. They understand that anxiety is that tiny prick that would irritate them for hours if they let it grow over them, and allow them to deviate from what they are meant to do.

How to conquer anxiety, then? Experts say that the best way is to stop procrastinating, and do what you are meant to do on time so that you do not extend your work till the last moment. At least they got one thing correct. Most of the time, last minutes are the ones that generate anxiety. This book addresses procrastination in the next chapter. When it comes to last minute work and anxiety, remember the old golden rule: 'Smart work'.

Making it clearer and quoting my brother, there are two kinds of work styles: hard work and smart work. You have five days to study for an exam. You can either toil hard in those 120 hours, cram all you can from textbooks and the internet, or you can do this:

1. Search for all previous year papers you can find (one-two hours).
2. Find out patterns. Note down the questions that appear again and again over the years (five hours).
3. Search for the answers of those questions, and related stuff (ten hours).
4. Study the hell out of them (twenty hours).

I am bad when it comes to maths, but thanks to a calculator, I found out that the total sums up to 36–37 hours. Compare these 120 hours and these 36–37 hours.

Notice how I said that I used calculator to add these simple digits. Yeah, I am that bad in mathematics. But I still managed to pass high school and college examinations easily. I did it just by following the smart work concept. I know that it's a bad example, but go ahead, try and see it for yourself.

During the period of anxiety, all you have to remind yourself constantly is to keep your mind alert and keep doing the smart work. Boil down your tasks. Break them into simpler components, and then, do what you are meant to do. You will find that ghost of anxiety present running away from you.

Another thing to remember is: to relax. Ease yourself. It is great to immerse into work but taking that sharp log of wood straight to your heart will just put you down. Lose yourself in your work, but sight of reality. When the time comes, when you are pulled by anxiety, you will know that things are conquerable and you just need to breathe.

Jerry Seinfeld, the great comedian had a chronic anxiety problem. Due to his anxiety to perform, the first time he walked on stage at a comedy club, he looked out at the audience, froze and was eventually jeered and booed off stage. Seinfeld knew he could do it, and he gave himself an entire day to relax. He went back the next night, completed his set to laughter and applause, and the rest is history.

People make great mistakes by trying hard to get themselves motivated through various things when they get anxiety attacks. It always ends up in making them agitated. The key is to remain calm and keep doing the work instead of pushing yourself. Do not let anxiety grow over you. It's your body and you cannot allow that rubbish to feed on you.

If we cut out the last minute thing and discuss conquering anxiety in general, it is all about good adrenaline and bad adrenaline. Simply put, good adrenaline is happiness and bad adrenaline is nervousness and anxiety. But hold on, there is a godsend for this. Video games. Or games in general.

Video games aren't meant for kids. I am not kidding. I am not telling you to buy expensive gaming consoles or a PC and those disks. I am asking you to pick up your phone and download anything that appeals to you and you can use your thumbs on. Video games are proven to curb the bad adrenaline level and they are one of the best ways to reduce anxiety. Don't want to download games on your phone, or don't have a phone? No problem. Buy the old handheld brick game thing that costs less than a magazine and it will be with you forever. Carry the device everywhere you go and play whenever you get an anxiety attack. Just play your anxiety out.

Hold on. You are an individual and have your own unique tastes, right? Maybe you one of those rare kind that hates video games and thinks of them as childish piece of shit. If you are then just do your stuff. Find out any of your interest that is 'portable' and use that. It may be books, magazines, hell even whistling or making weird noises with your armpits - just do it! Do whatever you love and keep yourself immersed in it to control your anxiety.

Another thing is positive self-talking. Positive self-talk is pretty important. It helps you fight the negative things you think of, fight the root reason for anxiety and fill yourself with some positivity. Some points on dealing with anxiety are:

1. Do not fear anxiety attacks. They will pass and will not kill you. One of the root causes of anxiety is the fear of anxiety itself.
2. Self-talk is crucial. Fight negative thoughts by filling yourself with positivity.
3. Do not indulge in hard work, instead, make sure to do smart work.
4. Breathe. Breathe a lot.
5. We are talking about general anxiety. If you have serious issues with anxiety, do not hesitate to go for professional help; either therapy or meditation.

Though it is hard to calm down during an anxiety attack, and even thinking of calming down isn't easy, with practice, you can do it smoothly. Communicate with your brain when you get an anxiety attack. Hell, you are the master. You can command your brain to calm down and listen, and it will, surely. With that, we will now dig a bit deeper into curbing anxiety. Let us list some of the known reasons behind anxiety and what to do when we get hit by them:

1. **Indecision**: Indecision is a main cause for anxiety. Most times, anxiety results from inner conflict. The key is to decide. Indecision is a big hindrance when you sit down to work. Decide and stay on whatever you have decided. One way to get yourself to decide is to assign affinity percentage to your choices. Say, you have a choice between working in daytime or at night. Quickly think of all the pros and cons, and then ask your brain about at which time it will be most productive. Then assign affinity percent to both day and night. If you have considerably more affinity towards a choice, stick with that choice.
2. **Stress**: The most obvious factor, stress, causes a lot of anxiety. When you are stressed, your brain overloads itself with pessimism and you start thinking that it will be hard to complete what you are doing. This makes you feel low and marks the beginning of the takeover of anxiety on you. To remove stress, there is no better answer than to 'relax'. Yeah, it is easy to read this word but difficult to apply, we know that. But we also know that we have to do it. Do not limit relaxing to television or reading or other means of leisure. Do what you want to do. As suggested before, whistle. Whistle your favorite tune. It may sound absurd but whistling has been proven to do wonders in bringing down stress levels. You can stretch your body for a while and try your hand at some mild exercises. Whatever you do, it must be simple and not frustrating. If you go for something frustrating or do something you don't do

to relax, things will not be easy and stress levels will shoot up again.

3. **Negative self-talk**: For most of us, anxiety is triggered by negative self-talking. As discussed, use positive self-talking to counter this. Try to replace negative self-talk with its positive counterpart. When you catch yourself thinking negatively, like, 'Damn, I can't do this, it's just too hard!' try to change it to something more positive, like, 'This maybe hard but I can get through it!' It can be helpful to think of plugging out the USB drive of anxiety that runs through your mind. Don't beat yourself up. Don't let that voice in your head say bad things about you. Anytime you hear yourself thinking 'You're a jerk, you can't get anything done. You won't succeed. People will make fun of you,' immediately, catch it and stop it dead in its tracks. Respond to your mental self-talk. Say, 'That's not necessarily true. There's no reason I can't get this done. I have to apply myself. Just because I screwed up once doesn't mean I'll always screw up. You're overreacting. Don't be ridiculous!' If you pay close attention to your negative part of mental self-talk, you will be amazed at how often it is criticizing you throughout the day. Shut it up.

4. **Change in aura**: Most of us start getting intimidated by a change in the routine. It maybe personal or due to things around you. This is perfectly normal as we are not usually used to change. With change, comes anxiety. We start getting worried about events and in the process find ourselves ridden with anxiety. To

overcome this, we need to increase adaptability. The only way we can do this is by convincing ourselves that where there change is inevitable. Change will be present throughout with us in any form. The sooner we start adapting, the sooner will we conquer over anxiety.

An anxiety attack is a release of bad adrenaline into the body. Your mind believes there is a threat so it releases adrenaline into your system. If the threat is a thing, you can overcome that. But if the threat is a thought, you can't run away from it. When your threats take over your thoughts, you are not in any actual danger but your body thinks it is and reacts accordingly. What can we do for this release of bad adrenaline?

Taking anxiety attacks as just a bad adrenaline flow is the key. When the attack starts, you will realize that the uncomfortable sensation is just adrenaline rushing around your body. It can't hurt you. Although it is uncomfortable, nothing can happen to you. The adrenaline will stop soon and you will feel better. Having an anxiety attack doesn't mean that anything is wrong with you; it is just the human body's way of dealing with a perceived threat. It is a normal fight-or-flight response.

Anxiety stems from our mind being too self-critical. Do you want to know why your mind is so self-critical? This is because of our thinking that there is something inherently wrong with us and that it must be controlled, tamed. Most people constantly overwhelm themselves by berating themselves for their past actions, or live in fear of some imagined worry. They keep piling on the guilt. The negative self-talk sets in here and takes root. 'I can't do this. I can't do that. I've tried this, and nothing is working. Nothing works, why can't I do even the most basic things? Nothing ever sticks. I always make the wrong decisions, why am I such a failure? I don't have any control over myself or my life, so why even try?'

Well, guess what? Your body is responding to your calls for help, and it's doing your bidding by starting to shut you down. Think about that for a moment. Is that really what you want? It can't do anything for you like this. It only works against you. You're programming your mind to give you more of the same opportunities to feel bad about yourself by activating your Reticular Activating System to actively seek out instances where you blame yourself, since this is what your body and mind interprets as your desire, as it's where you're primarily placing your emotionally dominant thoughts regarding these situations.

There is nothing inherently wrong with humans. Look at how eager children are to learn. This is true motivation. But that is ruined by how we are raised, to believe there is something wrong with us, which is actually what creates these issues of lack of motivation, procrastination and the like. We adopt the critical voices of others as our own.

What is missing here is self-compassion. The default state, the way we are born: our self-worth is inherent. We do not have to earn self-worth. We don't have to do anything. The most successful people are those who have let these harming beliefs and expectations go. They do it effortlessly, for the intrinsic reward, not for a critical voice.

Critical thoughts about ourselves trigger the body's stress response, causing a great deal of suffering and anxiety. There is no evolutionary benefit here. Other animals' fight or flight response get triggered as well, but as soon as the threat passes, they return to grazing or whatever else, as if nothing happened. Since we like to obsess over the past and identify memories instead of the only reality, this present moment, the stressful thoughts are regurgitated over and over again, continuing to cause the stress response and anxiety. The next time you are tempted by your bad thinking, embrace the temptation and overcome it, because overcoming that temptation is what will kick anxiety's ass.

Sometimes anxiety forces you to take quick actions without thinking. It forces you to do whatever the first case is during that time instant. This is not because it isn't giving you the time to think, this is because you are not identifying the time it is giving and not utilizing every moment of it. Here I will put a theory called two seconds of contemplating. No, this theory isn't as complicated as the name. I gave it such name just because it sounds good. Whenever you face anxiety, it gives you very little time to think before you act: say two seconds. In those two seconds, you have to think critically and make a decision about the choices, whether two or many.

What we do is, due to anxiety, we try to shift entire balance towards a choice. Anxiety puts us into an illusion that we need to be a hundred percent sure of our choice, and if not, we should simply act and go with the first nonsense that comes in our mind. It tries to do that in two seconds. Two-bloody-seconds. How can one think in those two seconds?

The answer to this is, instead of trying to get 100% sure about a choice, get inclined towards a choice that you like. Even a little inclination will do. To put it in simple words: during anxiety, do not over think. Go with the inclinations that you have always had. When you go with an inclination you always had, you will do better as you have must have thought about it before the state of anxiety. In those two seconds, just think of the inclination. This inclination will eliminate your anxiety.

But isn't that somewhat related to what anxiety is trying to do? Becoming inclined towards a particular choice instantly? No. Anxiety will try to get you inclined towards a random choice, passing by. You will not have any control in choosing, you will just follow that choice involuntarily. That is not expected from a champion. A champion follows his own choice, and what he is inclined towards no matter how hard anxiety tries.

What we have talked about here deals with anxiety in general. If you have a chronic case of anxiety, meditation and therapy sessions work a lot. Don't hesitate in exploring such options. Remember to keep hoping and stop giving a damn to anxiety.

Keep reading, champion.

Procrastination and Sloth

We'll begin with this: 'Avoid procrastination!'

Yeah, do it! It's easy. BAM. There you go! You have avoided it! End of chapter.

Bullshit.

You know, the phrase 'Avoid procrastination' is only good advice for people who don't really want to throw off procrastination. It is also good for people who say, 'I am always active on WTF: WhatsApp, Twitter and Facebook. Oh, I am such a procrastinator! And I must control it!' They are the very people who give free advice to people, 'Just do not procrastinate and do your work, you will do something good.'

It isn't good for people like us. People who can do things, but don't.

What's the difference between non-procrastinators and procrastinators? Both are perfectly sane human beings, capable of making quick decisions. Both have the power to control their brain. There is a single factor that separates both of them: Diversion.

Procrastinators show some weird traits. They have a brain that functions at a higher rate than others. This should act as a boon, but ends up as a curse.

You wake up. Brush, bathe, do your stuff. You sit down to work. You start working, yes you do. Suddenly, a topic strikes you out of nowhere. You look for it; think about it and Google it. You start with that topic and you end up watching top ten dangerous creatures in the deep sea on YouTube. Before you know it, the day ends. You tell yourself you will start again tomorrow.

Procrastination has to be conquered one way or the other. It hinders a champion's progress. Let us get started, right now. Let us talk about how to get working.

When you are about to sleep, write two important tasks for tomorrow. Ask yourself, what two things you can accomplish tomorrow that will make the biggest difference in your life. List them in order of importance. One and two. So you have your two tasks for the day. What you should do next is to break these tasks down into action steps, mentally. Let's say that your task is to write an article on something. Give yourself directions.

Let us write an article.

1. Find and read things related to that article.

2. Write down the components of the article.
3. Create a rough draft of the article
4. Format.
5. Proofread.

Well, that is it. Do you see the difference between 'writing an article' and the five steps listed? Breaking it down makes it a lot easier for you to follow.

Now, what about distractions? Someone pinged you on WhatsApp? Stop right there.

- Log out of Facebook. Scrolling up and down the news feed will only eat your time up.
- There's nothing that good on television that is more entertaining than living your life as someone great. Turn your television off.
- If you work on a computer, clean your desktop. If you are working on your table, clean it. Nothing should make you unfocused.
- Put your phone on vibrate and put it in another room or in your desk drawer.

Need a break? Do not waste it watching porn or other things. There is a guy called Francesco Cirillo who has a technique for you. It's called the 'Pomodoro technique'. You can Google it. It just asks you to work in increments of 25 minutes with 5 minute breaks. Or 50 minutes work, 10 minutes break. It depends on the kind of procrastinator you are.

Now let us address the worst problem. The wandering of your mind. The diversion. Sometimes you'll be in the minute of work and your mind just starts wandering, you're distracted, or you just don't want to work. You just have to do this:

1. Empty your mind.
2. Tell yourself something to keep working. Use expletives. STFU.
3. Picture yourself standing up on stage and telling your success story to everyone. Think of yourself giving interviews.
4. Get back to work and get closer to accomplishing your goals.
5. Just start whatever you are doing.

Being productive is a skill. Like all skills, it takes practice.

Let us say you want to be a good runner but you have been a couch-potato your whole life. Your goal should be to walk a mile first, and then slowly build upon your progress. You have to start, and that will ensure you that you will have your work done. If you have never done more than two hours of solid work before, tomorrow you should aim for two hours and 30 minutes. Then three hours and then four hours.

Marcus Aurelius, the Roman emperor, wrote in his book Meditations on getting out of bed:

'At dawn, when you have trouble getting out of bed, tell yourself: 'I have to go to work – as a human being. What do I have to

complain of, if I'm going to do what I was born for – the things I was brought into the world to do? Or is this what I was created for? To huddle under the blankets and stay warm?'

But it's nicer here.

'So you were born to feel nice? Instead of doing things and experiencing them? Don't you see the plants, the birds, the ants and spiders and bees going about their individual tasks, putting the world in order, as best they can? You're not willing to do your job as a human being? Why aren't you running to do what your nature demands?'

But we have to sleep sometime.

'Agreed. But nature set a limit on that – as it did on eating and drinking. And you're over the limit. You've had more than enough of that. But not of working. There you're still below your quota too, and what it demands of you. People who love what they do wear themselves down doing it, they even forget to wash or eat. Do you have less respect for your own nature than the engraver does for engraving, the dancer for dance, the miser for money or the social climber for status? When they're really possessed by what they do, they'd rather stop eating and sleeping than give up their arts. Is helping others less valuable to you? Not worth your effort?'

When this dude knew how procrastination sucks back in 167 A.C.E. and wrote on it, why don't we do something about it?

Don't make yourself worry about procrastinating and in that process, ruin your work. Understand that procrastination stops you from doing things you could have done to do something extraordinary. Looking at procrastination differently, if you start your day off with five minutes of surfing the internet, or television, the highly stimulating stuff you see will completely throw your brain into a state thinking about internet stuff, which makes it very difficult to now refocus on something which is slow and has a far-off payoff, versus the frenetic energy of the internet and television where your pleasure center's next reward is just a click and a button away. This means that those five minutes can easily turn into twenty minutes, which can turn into two hours, and then seven hours.

So what's the solution? Simply start your work immediately after waking, and definitely do not do anything highly stimulating and unproductive, unless you want your brain to get stuck in a dumbed-down state.

The idea is that once you start with Internet-television-Facebook-WhatsApp stuff, it is very unlikely that you will get back. Get your brain into a state of productivity as soon as you wake up, and start on whatever task you need to do within twenty minutes of waking up. This allows you to use the excess 'bouncing around' of ideas to your advantage, because now your brain will naturally be tilted towards working for the rest of the day, unless you ruin it.

Isn't it crazy that your scumbag brain will take something as trivial as checking a comment you posted to see if there were responses, and prioritize that as being more important than working so you can reach closer to your goal? Learn to stop being a douche bag and don't leave your dreams for later. Relish in your energy, your passions. Every time a task seems easily do-able or nearly finished, you will find yourself instantly relaxing and awarding yourself a break, even if you still have a long way to go until the end. How do you convince yourself to work and finish?

The simple answer for this would be that instead of rewarding yourself for an easy task, use any momentum you've gained to transit into a slightly more difficult and rewarding task that will actually make a break worth. You need to convert that momentum into productivity. Notice that I mentioned specific things like Facebook and television. Do not get this into your mind that they are the reason behind your procrastination. Think of a scenario. What if you have some papers to write and you are sent to a cabin in the woods with only your study material? No internet connection, no cell phone service, no television, no one to talk to. Just books and pages. Will you be able to complete your papers?

The answer may seem affirmative, but in practicality, it is not. You will still find ways to procrastinate. When it will be time to cook, you will cook for real, real long. You will take a lot of naps so you could focus. You will bath for a damn long time. You will look outside the window and keep staring at something trivial. You may even start planning and plotting but not actually do your job.

The point is that procrastination has nothing to do with your external environment. It's an internal issue, one that can be hard to pin down. You can download all the time management software in the world, Google and memorize all the tips on the internet and still procrastinate. The key is to address the triggers that cause the behavior, not the circumstances that allow it. It is your brain that does that. Do not allow it to wander.

Procrastination can be viewed as a combination of influences. It goes like: 'I should stop doing my work now - there is something more fun to do - I can do it tomorrow - it doesn't NEED to be done now – it is too big of a task - it overwhelms me, or I'm too tired.'

To overcome this you can use that age old 'one step' process. Don't think about washing all the dishes; just go do one dish. That's it. It will help get you over the hurdles in your mind. It will make your brain go like: 'It goes quickly, it is not difficult or too big to do, if I start it I can stop at any time.'

You will find that the actual hurdle has been overcome, that is getting started. We often are creatures of momentum. We enjoy continuing to do what we are doing, even if it is not the most enjoyable thing in the world. And that generates the procrastination bugs.

Can't find the motivation to go for a run? Then don't think of it as a run, just throw on your running gear and take the first step - then see what happens. That second, then third step, they come much more easily, as part of the task is already in the past.

Can't find the motivation to write? Just write a page, then two, then three, then four. You will find that, you are already there; it is not much more effort to write some more pages.

Whatever it is that you are procrastinating, just figure out what the first real step is and make that your goal. When you will overcome the first step, the rest of it will become much easier. Take the step.

Imagine one day you pick up the phone and are offered an incredible job in New Delhi. They will put you up there in lodgings, company car, six-seven figure salary, and you basically do nothing but make the chimps under you do all the work. The only problem is that you live in Jaipur, around 270 Kilometers away from your destination. And you don't have money to travel. Now if you sit on your ass and feel bad for yourself, you already lose. But if you start walking to Delhi, every step you take is one step closer to that amazing opportunity. And who along the way someone may offer you some small job that would fetch you some money to take a bus. Or you could even take a lift. That is not the point how you may reach after you take the first step. The point is that if you take that first step, you will reach Delhi. But you will never know, never have the chance to know that, until you take the first step out of your door. That first step is one step closer to Delhi.

Take your first step because it does wonders. This small yet hard decision will be a true game changer in your life. You don't have to look at the entire path and tell yourself it is too long. The plain, simple logic is that the minute you take your first step, your path will seem smaller.

Moving onto another reason behind procrastination, let us talk about analysis paralysis. Nope, that is not the name of a punk rock album. So what is analysis paralysis? Wikipedia on this term goes: Analysis paralysis is the state of over-thinking a situation and doing it so much that a decision or action is never taken, in effect paralyzing the outcome. A decision can be treated as over-complicated, with too many detailed options, so that a choice is never made, rather than try something and change if a major problem arises.

Analysis paralysis is over thinking so much, that you start getting obsessed over an issue and then you are unable to move beyond it. You start procrastinating. When you get struck by analysis paralysis during your work, you can't make any forward progress because you bog yourself down in brainstorming about the issues and details. You bog yourself down in planning and plotting so much, that you forget that you actually have to put your thoughts to work. You aim on your targets, but while aiming you forget that you have to hit the target.

Another thing is you get paralyzed by the possibility of failure. To counter that possibility of failure, you start envisioning success. For example, you may envision yourself getting into a top engineering college. Well that is pretty great that you are thinking about your future. But then you may get indulged in your fantasies to the point where you start deluding your own reality. In the case of envisioning about engineering college, you may start deluding your reality and not actually start studying. That is procrastination to avoid failure despite simultaneously inching towards it.

The real deal is about how to counter it. You can counter this by focusing on a deeper why level. Now what is this *why* level?

The *Why* level is the level of questioning yourself. We respond to *why*. Before you embark on a task, ponder about first why you want to do it. It has to hit you on a deep emotional and mental level, because if you're not fully bought into the process on an internal level, all your external show of discipline will evaporate in days if not hours. The first thing you need to do is come to making a decision. The just stop there, block your mind from thinking about that anymore because you already have an answer, and start doing your work. This will surely eliminate analysis paralysis and give you a start for your work.

We really need to do something about this decision making crap. No decision-making is really a big reason for procrastination and our work not being completed. In fact, it is one of the major reasons for bad days. Let us read about another interesting analogy. It isn't even an analogy; it is something obvious put in words. It is called the Aye-Nay theory, or simply the Yes-No theory.

Simply put, we get through the day simply by making a series of decisions, yes or no. The outcome of those decisions turn out to be positive, or negative. Bad days result from saying no to a majority of things you are supposed to do. Good days come from choosing a majority of positive decisions.

It is a pretty simple concept. An example for this is the first decision that most of us make at the start of the day; to press or not to press the snooze button on our alarm. Either we say yes, press the button, get up, and kick start our day or we hit snooze and keep dozing off.

After waking up, most of us will then have some breakfast and need to decide on eating the healthy food or the not so healthy, but delicious option. The latter will probably be bad for our healthy, give us less energy, and make us feel guilty for eating it and so on. But, we still pick the bad side of the yes-no decision to fulfill our need for instantaneous happiness, despite knowing it will be detrimental to us in the long run. And so these yes-no decisions carry on throughout the day, most of us picking the bad side every time.

Of course, the good decision is completely obvious most of the time. Eat some fruits or a family size bag of Lays for a snack? Get to the study table or mindlessly continue watching television? We all know this and we're all guilty of it. So how can we turn it around and use this concept to our benefit?

Well, we have to get out of the long term mentality and into the short term, present mentality. Sounds kind of counter-intuitive, right? What I mean by this is instead of thinking 'I'll treat myself with an unhealthy meal now and eat some vegetables later' change your thinking to 'I'm going to eat the vegetables now rather than the bad, unhealthy meal.'

By thinking for the short term, the obviousness of the decision you need to take becomes even more apparent. You simplify the yes-no decision you need to make by eliminating the shitty excuses you make to yourself, insinuating that you will make up for this bad decision now by doing something good later on, which, we know is unlikely to happen. So, in essence, we need to simplify these decisions to their most basic form, hence making it extremely easy to pick the right option.

Don't overcomplicate every decision by saying things like 'I'll just check Facebook for 5 minutes and get straight to work afterwards.' This kind of thinking leads to bad decisions because you are trying to convince yourself that you will *responsibly procrastinate* for a small amount of time and then get on with your work, when you definitely won't. You won't even know and those five minutes will turn into hours. Instead of overcomplicating like the above example, simply ask yourself 'Work or Facebook? Being a champion or spend time liking useless posts and typing hip things as status updates?'

Instantly the decision becomes much easier as you have eliminated excuses and lies you use to trick yourself. You know that you can't procrastinate responsibly and hence you don't try to trick yourself that you will, saving yourself from wasting a lot of precious time needlessly and taking the positive, beneficial route instead. Now let us slightly deviate from this topic. There are people who do not procrastinate, but their work doesn't just complete on time. This is because they spend time resting their ass off. They know they have work, they want to do it. But they do not do it.

The reason? Laziness. Slothing. Is 'slothing' a word? Yeah, it is. But again, champions don't sloth around.

Let us look at this problem and its solution another way round. Yes. There are days when you don't want to get off the bed/couch. There are days when you just do not want to work. Let us call these days, null days. What is a null day? A null day is a day when you do not do anything towards your goals. Tell yourself to have no more null days. No!

Do not push yourself. No one is asking you to do some big labors to eliminate the null days. Let us say, you are writing a paper. So no one is telling you to write the paper at one go, in a day. Say, it is night, and you haven't done anything the entire day. So, write a word, a sentence, whatever you can just to ensure you are moving a small step towards completing that paper. Never waste a day. Stick this on your wall. **No Null Days**.

Enter another problem for null days. How do you pick yourself back up when your mind has convinced you to be lazy today, or for the next couple days? That's a problem you will run into a lot, where your mind will just convince you that your couch is more comfortable, or you can start that project tomorrow, and other stuff.

Remember that it is all about those two words: Aye or Nay. Yes or No. Choose yes, always. Because champions choose yes. Because you want to be a champion and you can be one. So now you know how to put a full stop to procrastination. Now enters another thing that screws with your time; sloth. Laziness.

The problem with laziness is, well, you know that you are lazy. You know that being a lazy asshole isn't good. But still you cannot do anything about it because you are too lazy to think and do something about your laziness. Yeah, that hurts to read. But it is true in every way. Laziness is the most stubborn enemy that a person who is on the path of becoming a champion faces. It is because you can do whatever you want to remove it from the path, it will reappear and stop you. If it doesn't stop you, it will divert you.

Hold on a second. Divert? How does laziness divert? Isn't it supposed to be only a hindrance?

Well, no. When you start feeling lazy while doing a work, you become a completely different person doing that work. Let us call this sloth attack. When you get a sloth attack (start feeling lazy) you start thinking of various ways to complete that work. That may even include ways that don't actually complete that work, but they complement your laziness and look good.

Need an illustration? Let's say you want to ride a bicycle.

Now, you hit the internet and books. You go through the internet forums with people who talk about how they learned and read about the subject. You study the gears, efficiency and air pressure. Every little component. Time passes and you turn out to be well versed in the idea of bicycle. After all that time, can you ride one? Nope. You know that the true way to learn to ride a bicycle is to get on the bicycle, start pedaling, fall off and try again, and again. On the other hand, children can learn to ride but not understand half of the physics that went into its understanding.

That is how laziness deludes you. It leaves you inside a maze that ends up in nothingness or most of the times it ends up in halting your work completely. The consequences of sloth attacks are always the worst. It is not exactly your fault if you are lazy. The thing is that we are born with laziness. Everyone is lazy by nature, as we naturally want to conserve energy. But to allow that laziness to grow on you with time and not eliminating when it needs to be eliminated is the thing that will cause great problems.

Most people seeking advice to change their life know exactly what to do. The problem is, they don't feel like going through the process. So they go looking for a magic method, an 'aha' moment, or some sort of sentence that will magically scramble their brain into place. But that isn't right. People that enjoy success don't sit around and wait for the feeling of dedication. They simply act while others twiddle their thumbs. Sure, you may not feel like doing what you have to. But that is only because you have already made the decision that you should stop and do your work later.

Now you have to decide how far you want to pursue success. You have to power through those intense moments of not feeling like doing something.

We all know what we have to do in life to get to where we want to be, for the most part. It's just a matter of sucking it up and putting in work at the times when we least feel like it.

A majority of the people don't rise up against themselves, even though we are all facing that daily battle. Champions know what it takes and are willing to sacrifice feeling good for obtaining goals.

You know this. At times, you go lazy because of a reason. Your negative side wants you to be like every other guy on the street. Will you let yourself be that? Or will you exert the power you hold over yourself and grab hold of the reins and work for your victory? Your choice.

Another thing that sprouts laziness is that sometimes you become unclear of what you want to do. You don't have a definite way to go. To counter this, what you need is a structure. You can't stay disciplined without a vision of what it is you are striving towards. From these goals, you need plans that you can execute through daily habits. In short, you need to know what to do and why to do it. This is a great tactic to eliminate laziness. Remember, most times motivation will not help you patch up your lazy habits. You may be motivated but that doesn't necessarily mean you are not lazy. Laziness is eliminated smoothly and delicately. It doesn't necessarily require force.

How do you get over sloth attacks, now? Let us break the solution down into points:

1. Never force yourself: This isn't about motivation or making yourself ready to work by brute force. Instead of forcing yourself, mold your work in a way that you enjoy doing it. Let us take the example of running. A run can be painful drudgery, or a lovely time clearing your head and enjoying the outdoors. You won't get very far doing anything if you have to force yourself every day.
2. Pick up the momentum and use that: Once you start, keep your momentum turned on and keep going. This again is a matter of how you mold things. Once you get hold of the pace, never lose your momentum and keep working with all you have.

3. Remember the bit-by-bit rule: Increase your work gradually. Throwing yourself full force into something might work for a small run, but it also makes it hard to keep showing up every day. Start small, and each day, just show up. Gradually increase what you do, so that each step along the way it still feels easy and fun.
4. Remember, laziness will hinder your progress towards becoming a champion: You're doing the work presumably because you want to do it. You want to show it to the world who you are. You want to become a champion. When we stop doing something, it is because we have forgotten that we wanted it. We start to repel it for some reason, and try not to think about it. The key is to think about it and remind yourself of why you started doing it in the first place.

Most times, laziness results from distractions and losing focus. For this, the American author, Jack Kornfield has this amazing analogy between training a dog and training the mind to focus. When you start training a dog, the first thing you do is take it to a mat and tell it to, 'Sit. Stay.' At first the dog won't even sit, but you don't give up and you don't shout at it, you just keep bringing it back to the mat and guiding it to sit. If you shout at the dog you don't get an obedient dog, you get a disobedient dog that's afraid of you.

Once you get the dog to sit, you walk away. Probably the dog will get up and follow you. At this point, do you give up? Do you shout at the dog? No. The same rules apply. You gently guide it back to the mat and tell it, 'Sit.

Stay.' Eventually, with persistence, the dog learns to stay for a few seconds, then a few minutes and then however long until you call it to come.

In the same way, when we focus, we tell the mind, 'Stop. Focus.' and sooner or later, the mind will wander. Now just stop. You should not use this as an excuse to quit or berate yourself for being weak. Minds wander, that's their nature, and forcing yourself won't change it. You stop and curse the mind every time you don't do something; you get a mind that associates that thing with the negative feeling of being cursed. The result will be even more resistance. One shouldn't go for that.

The thing about this analogy is that it's applicable to everything that involves concentration or focus. Whenever you find that you're not focused on what you should be focused on, whenever you slip from following your goals, you don't waste time beating yourself up. You just gently bring the dog back to the mat. The more you practice both starting and restarting an activity and sticking with an activity, the easier it gets. Eventually, focusing becomes so easy that you will not even notice that you're doing it.

A small thing about laziness that we need to know is that laziness is not cool. Some try to *show-off* their laziness. They probably do it because they want to show their friends that they have a lot of leisure time and so they are hipsters. They do it as 'Oh! I am so lazy. If I weren't so lazy, I would have done great at things!' This is cringe-worthy. One, you are telling the world about one of your flaws. Two, laziness is for immature boys and girls; not for men and women. Treat laziness as a threat, not something light enough to laugh-off.

You just have to pick yourself up at the very moment you are falling back to rest and tell yourself that you have to do your job. It is time for taking a rational look at laziness. Human beings are animals, built to survive. On earth, millions of different animals have lived and died, with one shared goal, survival. It took about thousands of years for our species to figure stuff out, but human beings got really good at survival. Suspiciously good. And we really began to thrive. Every second of human progress has built up to this day, and provided us with our relatively lavish, modern existence. This is a day and age where you never have to think about survival, and that I can say because you are able to at least read these lines as of now.

Now your problem is that you are not 'making it big', right? But you're smart enough to understand that there is a problem in the first place, which is good. A simple answer to your query is to acknowledge this era. This is an era where knowledge, compassion and creativity are cherished on a scale never seen before on Earth. No animal in the Earth's 4.5 billion year history has had as much potential to wake up the next day, and watch, listen, travel, read, feel, create, help, sing, play or love as you do. So, you do have your potential. No problem there.

Looking at other people's success? That's easy. Listening to people talk about their success? That's easy. Changing yourself and stop being lazy? That's hard. It's the hardest thing you can possibly do. There is one fact that that is entirely true, and it is that you have literally everything you need to make yourself the best you can possibly be. Hold on right there. Yes, you have the potential. Now let us face the reality. Every other person thinks they are some lazy genius and it is because of their schooling that they did not use their full potential.

But, that potential doesn't mean shit if you don't get off your ass and start working. When you start labeling yourself as a lazy genius, that label literally becomes how you define yourself. Your self-confidence, how you look at yourself in the mirror, all of it, is based on the fact that you think of yourself as 'lazy genius'. Now, you unconsciously make the assumption that genius people don't work hard. Genius people should just get it. And since you're genius, you shouldn't have to work hard. So you don't. If you had to work hard, that means you aren't genius and your entire self-image comes crashing down. Now, what should we do for this?

The answer to this question is to redefine your definition of genius. You think genius is something along the lines of IQ. Being born genius means you have everything and you will surely succeed even if you are damn lazy. That's not what smart means. That's not what being smart is all about. You need to start equating the word genius with the term doer. You just need to ditch your self-definition that relies on being labeled genius and realize that intelligence is meaningless without work. Remember that genius people are only those who know the value of working and not being lazy.

You must repel laziness from within. This repulse to laziness cannot be taught. Only you can ask this laziness to get the hell away from yourself. I can't pick you up out of your god damn chair. I can't buy you whatever you think will make your life better until you inevitably give up and go back to the old ways.

That's right! This book can motivate you to work. This book can motivate you to get up at 5 am and go running. This book can motivate you to do your chores. Then what? At some point you will put down this book, and you will decide that this whole change thing was a whole lot harder than you bargained for. You may follow other things in this book, but whenever it will come to laziness, you will slowly recede back to your old lazy self. That's why you need to be your motivation.

Don't lie around like a lazy ass because you worked up a sweat yesterday and deserve today off. To hell with yesterday! Yesterday was a weaker you. It's time to get up and make today the weaker you for tomorrow. That isn't this book's job. This is yours. You're not special because of what you did today. You're special because of what you do every single day. Be the person who gets all the work complete. Be the person with all promises fulfilled. Be the person that has all shit under control. Be the person who can never be called lazy.

Procrastination and laziness will always screw you up and put you in the midst of a lot of troubles. They seem to be pretty normal, common problems but are as worse as any other. Be a worker and things will always turn out to be just like how you want. Never let these two things be your weak points.

Keep reading, champion.

About You

People spend their lifetime thinking about just one question:

'Who am I?'

When this strikes, they forget everything else that is relevant. They read books, philosophical journals, develop a profound interest in philosophy and whatnot. This stage is technically called the existential crisis. It is scary, and helps you know your purpose and what you want to do in life. The existential crisis is great. It puts the cogwheels in your brain working and makes you think about your life. But what if this existential crisis comes late in your life?

What if you cross 60, and you find that you never did anything relevant? Or that you never found out the answer to who you are? What if you cross 60 and you find that you wasted an entire lifetime being things you never wanted to be? What if you find that you were imitating others throughout life? It would be the worst nightmare of your life.

Can this be avoided? Aye.

There is only one answer to this. Finding out who you are, and being that person. Well, that is a bad answer. A clearer version of it is: Create your own persona. We have discussed this before. You are born with unique traits and set of skills that only you possess. What you have to do now is to build yourself around that. We need to build an identity.

What is identity? In simple words, your identity is a fixed thing. By being that fixed thing, you will be someone walking on the path towards greatness. Think of your identity as an empty bottle where you keep pouring liquids till the concentration is right. There is something that is mildly annoying and confusing. We know about 'change'. We know that change is inevitable. And this change doesn't spare even your identity or who you are. The truth is, who we are changes over time, so trying to 'be yourself' is like shooting for a moving target. There is a counter for this: improve who you are, not be who you already were. Improve your present to directly interfere with and improve your future.

That said, our identities are not infinitely malleable. If you try to be something that is far from what you currently are it will feel fake and make you unhappy. For building an identity, you will have to win a small war. This war is against those parts of you that are stupid, malevolent, and unseemly. Those parts must be fought and suppressed until they are defeated. Always remember, you are meant to be something better. There are infinitely many good things about you that separate you from people. Those should be maximized without holding back.

Let us do an exercise. Try to create a mental picture of yourself. Probably the picture your brain will create would be of some photograph of yours, so let us change that. Imagine yourself standing on a stage behind a podium while a massive crowd is looking at you, waiting for you to speak and the paparazzi is all around flashing cameras at you. Now stop right there and take a closer look at yourself. What do you have right now that will put you on that stage? Think of your existing good traits. Are you honest? Hard working? Great learner? Observer? Thinker? If not, what possibly can make this scenario happen in real life? What things do you need to learn to make this scenario come true? Imagine yourself in any scenario, the one you badly want to happen. Then think of the things you are lacking to be able to make it to there.

Story time. Here is another anthropomorphic animal story to explain things clearly:

A parrot called Bart came home upset. His mother asked him, 'What happened, Bart?'

'I hate my goddamn beak!' Bart blurted.

'Why do you hate your beak? I think it is beautiful.' his mother said reassuringly.

'All of the other birds have much cooler beaks. Maggie spoonbill, Lisa pelican, Millhouse hawk, Krusty finch, all of them!'

Bart's mother sat silently for a moment. 'He may be right,' she thought to herself, 'they do have awesome beaks.'

'You should see Homer. He'll know what to do. He's the wisest of the parrots and lives in the tallest tree in the forest,' said Bart's mother.

Bart flew to the tallest tree in the forest and found Homer the parrot.

'Excuse me, Homer, I have a problem!' said Bart.

'And that is?' asked Homer.

'I have a stupid beak. Why can't I have a cool beak like Maggie spoonbill, Lisa pelican, Millhouse hawk or Krusty finch?'

'You're right.' said Homer, 'They do have cool beaks. Tell me Bart, do you like eating worms and crustaceans?'

'Yuck! That would be disgusting!' responded Bart.

'Well, that's what the spoonbill's beak is designed for. What about fish?'

'I couldn't think of anything worse.' said Bart.

'So, the pelican's beak would work either.'

'What about rabbits and mice?'

'Damn it!'

'Okay, so maybe you shouldn't aspire to have a hawk's beak. Do you like small seeds?'

'They are awesome, but my favorite is Brazil nuts.' exclaimed Bart, salivating at the thought.

'That is lucky; I think I have a few here. Would you like one?' asked Homer.

Bart's eyes lit up. 'Yes, please.'

'Tell me Bart, if you had the beak of a spoonbill, pelican, hawk or finch, do you think that you could eat that Brazil nut?'

'I guess not!' said Bart with his mouth full.

'You see, young parrot, you have been designed a certain way, with certain skills, attributes and tastes. Don't waste your life being envious of the capacities of others. Just make sure that you know what you're good at and why you're here.'

Bart nodded in understanding and flew back home, content.

Again, there is no moral of this story. What we need to know here is that when you are yourself, you have greater possibilities to work on your skills. Now we will talk on how to define your identity. First, accept yourself. If you really want to be a champion, it is time to throw off any masks you are wearing. Here is a fact: you cannot hide any crevices in your personality by faking it. People get impressed only by how you deal with your imperfections. Show yourself who you are, and be that person.

Do you feel uncomfortable wearing particular clothes that are fashionable? Throw them off, wear your tee and put on whatever you are comfortable in. Do you like it better when you eat with your hands rather than use a spoon? Do it. Do you like to watch cartoons rather than popular western shows and sitcoms? Do it. Do everything the way you want to instead of faking it merely to get approval from your peers. If the face you always show the world is a mask, someday there will be nothing beneath it.

But maybe another question has risen in your mind, how can you 'keep being yourself' when you have to improve in order to become a champion?

The problem is that we keep getting confused when we are told to 'change for better' and 'accept yourself the way you are'. We think that both statements contradict each other, though they don't. When we are talking about accepting ourselves the way we are, we talk about the general sense and traits of our personality. We talk about how we actually are instead of borrowing others' attitudes and personas. We talk about our own traits and skills. When we talk about changing for better, we are talking about improving and using the skills we already have, and learning skills that will complete our character and identity. Now, think of celebrities or characters you have worshipped throughout your life. Small or big, think of everyone. Was there any point in life when you tried to be like them? Tried to copy their mannerisms or things they did? Do those habits continue till date? The thing we are talking about here is that one word called influence.

Throughout life, you have influences. Your peers, elders, people you know, celebrities, many have influences on you at a period of time or the other. It doesn't matter if you are 10 or 32. You will be impressionable throughout your lifetime. That is pretty normal. The thing you have to know is about good influences and bad influences. Keep in mind that we are not talking about good or bad company here. We are talking about effect someone has on your behavior.

You know everything about both type of influences, you just need to distinguish them from one another. Influences from people should be limited to good, positive vibrations and qualities. How? When you feel that something a person does is nice, do not immediately get influenced by it, stop for a split second and think it from your perspective if it will benefit you. That particular thing which the respective person does may be good for him but may not prove fruitful for you. If you find that it is indeed fruitful for you, allow yourself to get influenced by it. And you can definitely allow yourself to get influenced. All you have to do is see things rationally.

This is good influence. The key is not to jump to conclusions by seeing something from others' view-frame. You should judge and decide if that thing is good for you. Bad influence results from blindly following what others do. Never force yourself to live like a celebrity you admire. Look forward to your own adventure. You are not Brad Pitt, you are not Barack Obama, you are not Ellen DeGeneres, you will never be and you should not try to be. But yeah, you can be above them. You are your own master, and you can walk the road you want to walk. Ask yourself: 'What keeps me from doing exactly what I want to?' The most likely answer is: 'Myself.' Don't try to live up to others, but make your own adventure.

We have talked about effects people may have on you, but there is a paradox is about learning from others' behaviors that is confusing. They say that you should learn nice things from every person you meet. That is great. Many do that, but end up imitating others. What you should do is not to try too hard to learn nice things, but study the bad things. The worst parts of every person you meet. Then, look into yourself and search if you have anything similar within you. Learn from the mistakes of others. Learn from their worst parts and how they affect them. With this process, you will end up with immense knowledge of 'what not to do.' And this knowledge will be important at every point in your life. Learning from fools and mistakes others do is the smartest thing. When you know what not to do, you have more confidence, clearer goal and clearer path with fewer obstacles. Moreover it makes your persona and cleanses you.

Now that we are talking about others, let us talk about people we know. Somewhere, most of you agree with this: relatives mostly suck. Most of them are simply there to criticize your actions. Others are examples. They are the examples given to you by your elders, peers, even your parents. They are much more successful than many around you and you are asked to follow their footsteps. And the truth is many start following. Probably because of the peer pressure they can't handle, but many start living in the shadows of their successful cousins, uncles or whomever they are given the examples of. But champions do not start under others' shadows.

You first have to start where you are at. You are not your cousin or uncle. You are a completely separate person with different wants and needs and while people you love may push you or guide you in a direction, it's up to you to take it at some point. Another thing to know is that people cannot impart success on you; it is something that comes from within. Do you feel that your peers have a dominating impact on you? Do they keep giving you examples? Are those examples generating different fears in you? Are those examples and whatever they are saying, mocking, or ridiculing you are deterring you from your path? If yes, let us do the only 'interactivity' thing this book will ask from you.

Take a sheet of plain paper. The biggest you can find. Take a marker. If you don't have one, even a normal pen will do. Scribble just three words on that page.

'PROVE THEM WRONG.'

Do not do write it in beautiful handwriting or calligraphy crap, write it in your handwriting. Now take the paper and paste it in your room, at a place where you can see it clearly whenever you are doing your work.

What will happen? What will these three words do? They will put your ass to work. When you see these three words, remind yourself that you have to prove those people and all that they said wrong. These three words should remind you of every word they said against you. These three words should remind you of every comparison that was made against you. These three words will push you towards your goal. Remember if people are trying to push you down, you can actually gather a lot of strength to push yourself up and further.

An old dog fell into a dry well. He started barking aloud expecting that someone will pull him out of the well. There were few passersby, who looked into the well and found the dog in a bad shape. They had no tools or ropes to pull him out. There was no help available around. Some smarter ones decided that the dog should die rather than troubling anyone to bring him out. Their argument was different though. According to them, in any case the dog didn't stand a chance of survival.

So, they collected the mud lying around and started throwing it into the well to bury the dog. Every time the mud was thrown at him, the dog shook the mud off his body and stepped on it. By the time the mud completely filled the well, the dog climbed the mud and came out of the well.

If someone throws mud at you, just shake it off yourself and get over it soon. Keep focusing on your goal and don't be distracted by what others believe. At some instant or the other, you will prove them wrong.

By now, you must have noticed that this book keeps touching the theme of revenge subtly. This is because mild revenge is good revenge. Some revenge is to be taken instead of being forgotten and this is one of them. Show the world what you can do and who you are. Show the world that you have a distinct identity. The world will try to push you back. Don't let the world win.

Different people have different opinions about who one should prove his worth to: himself or the people. Some say it is more important to prove to yourself what you can do and to hell with the public opinions, and some say it is better to prove it to those people who treat you inferior. But why not prove to both of them? Why can't you prove your worth to yourself as well as to the world? To prove your worth, you need to have a well-built, well-established identity. You need to conquer yourself before setting out to conquer others. No personality development or advices will help you if you are reluctant to make a distinct identity. With seven billion people and counting, this place needs more distinct and different people with their own persona.

Work on your own skills. You cannot learn something that you do not want to do but you have seen someone else doing it and you found that it looks great. Again, everyone has their own strengths and that is the very basis of making an identity.

Here is a little secret: You define your own ethics. There is no good or evil in this world. It is just a matter of perceiving how you should succeed. Yes, killing, stealing and doing other dishonorable acts are surely something a champion can never condone. But there are a few things which are perceived by the world wrongly. We have talked about things like anger and pain. But there are qualities like selfishness and egoism which have their meaning lost in present scenario.

When we talk about these two words, selfishness and egoism are not meant to be taken in a way people take them. When you are in the process of making your identity, you have to add a hint of both selfishness and egoism. The reason? One of the greatest bullshit in this world goes: 'Try to match steps with the world and you shall progress with the world around you.' Wrong. Why do you have to follow the world and match steps when you can lead the way? Remember that the people around you are not breathing in your body, you are. You have to take care of that body. You have to lead it towards the end of the path of being a champion. If you really want to do this, give priority to yourself. Give priority to yourself and you will find out that things will go in your favor. The point made here is; it is great to think about others. It is great to be kind enough to give others priority. But it is utterly foolish to do small favors to others sacrificing your time and yourself. Everyone wants to do favors to others be loved, but that doesn't mean you should lose respect and make others perceive you as a daily jobber. This will hurt your identity. Think for yourself first, and then if you have some time left help others. Stop viewing selfishness as something vile. Selfishness is nothing but an unorthodox quality.

Now we will talk about love. Okay, don't cringe looking at the word. But this is some mumbo jumbo bullshit. What is the word 'love' doing in a self-help book? This isn't a romantic novel. Isn't this a book for and about champions? So what relevance does love hold here? This is a legitimate question. But it is flawed. The problem is, we have grown up on movies, novels and the aura around us has led us to believe that every time the word 'love' pops up, it has to be associated with romance. But like many words, they are not the same. They are just interrelated as romance being a subtype of love. While romance is concerned mostly with the gestures of showing love, love is a strong feeling of affection or passion. It may even denote a great interest in something.

The love we are talking about is being passionate. It is being invested in your goal so much that you do not think of anything else but that goal. This goal you are passionate about, or putting it in better words, this goal you start loving may be anything ranging from that girl you know to being a Wall Street giant. If you want anything to work for you, you have to give in whatever you have. That is possible by loving a particular thing. When passion is combined with strength, anything you desire will always come to you. Invest in whatever you want to do, and be the person who loves doing whatever he does.

The point is to be comfortable with what you do and what you say, and what you wear. You may go ahead and wear a new fashionable thing or a dirty rug, but the point is to pull it off with confidence. For that, you must choose the one you find yourself most comfortable in. You may speak in any accent but that must be your own, not Morgan Freeman's or Liam Neeson's. Your accent, your clothes and your work must be in your own attitude and your way.

Another small thing to remember about you is, you are what you do. That is, you build yourself by the actions or the work you do. We have touched this topic before; let us understand this now in detail and a little theoretically.

The Slovenian philosopher Slavoj Zizek talked about something great in one of his lectures. He started off with examples. The first example he gave was that if you ask an adolescent boy about his father you will often get something about how stupid the father is in what a pretty typical adolescent rebelliousness. But when you observe that child around his father, you see a completely different story, one where the child shows some combination of respect, fear and love for his father. So which is the lie, the world in which that boy lives or the world in the boy's head?

Zizek used many more examples, but one more that was hard-hitting was the idea of soldiers at war. A Jew-killing Nazi may have been torn apart by the acts he was committing and barely able to live with himself. But does that in any way change the monster he is?

The idea here is that who we are is rooted in our actions. The story in our head, the world around us and everything else are abstractions of this most fundamental realm of existence. Damn, that's crazy. Okay, let us put this down simply.

How many times do you find some excuse not to work? Or not to study or not to give something my all and still retained the idea that 'you put in everything in doing your work; it is just that you don't want to do it today'? You are the same person who was doing the work before, right? But then, how can the same person say that he doesn't want to work now?

You are not some person that lives in your head. You are what you do. And every time you fail to act, you become that failure to act - no matter what lie you want to tell myself in my head.

Have you sat on Facebook for a few hours today, doing nothing else? If yes, you can make up any story you want in your head about how it is raining outside or that you need a relaxing day, but the fact is that you spent hours on Facebook today, doing nothing. Period. There is no story or context, just the fact of your actions - that is who you are.

When you will realize this, you will no longer tell yourself that you have to do some special thing tomorrow to be something. You will do it today. If you want to be rich you don't have to get organized, or become organized. You must be organized. If you want to do something, instead of making up an excuse, do it. That isn't something that you choose to do one day as a chore, it's not a switch you turn on when you need it - it's something you do or don't do through your actions, every day.

One thing to be careful of is not to define yourself by what you have not done. Just stick with the actions. Not going for a jog and sitting on WhatsApp doesn't make you someone who didn't go for that jog. You are someone who sat on WhatsApp.

If you define yourself by everything you are not, it is too easy to fall into a pattern of negativity in your thoughts. It is a form of self-abstraction used to feel better about yourself in the short term by having the illusion that you are just an observer. Make your choice and own it because that is who you ultimately are, your actions. Now that you know the small things that you need to build your own identity with, let us move on to something else. There is an entity which is periodically mentioned throughout this book. We are talking about people.

What about them? Who are they in your life? Aren't they meant to be ignored? Well, aye and nay. However hard we try, we will always find people affecting our life in a positive way or the other. As for the lives of champions, they do not try to block the influences of people, but they alter it in whatever way they want.

But isn't this chapter about us? Why should we spare our time to talk about people? Well, because we need to know a thing or two about people. We need to know them so that they can act as a catalyst for us to become a champion. Don't act surprised, we have already discussed doing that in the previous chapters. We have learnt to channel our anger towards people. We have learnt to let them throw down a challenge to us and then answer them by winning the hell out of it. Now what?

Now we will learn to dominate people. You must be thinking, 'Easy there, Satan!' But no, this isn't 'Dominate your meek peers in illicit ways for your own personal benefits', this is 'Dominating people you don't really have an attachment to.'

What will dominating others do to help you? Simply put, when you start dominating others, their negative influence over you reduces significantly and there will be only positive ones. Dominating others is simply keeping yourself ahead of others in the race and making people aid you on the way. Champions dominate, and they have to. Domination is a distinct characteristic of a champion. There is only one rule for domination, however. You must only try to dominate those who are on the same level as you are, intellectually, physically, or anything, depending upon your field. It is futile and cowardly to dominate over people who are much lower than you in life.

How do you do this? One line mantra: think like a dictator, act like a kind king. Cunningness isn't as bad as people make it out to be. It is really a handy quality to have if used, well, cunningly! When we are talking about dominating people, first of all we have to talk about winning over them. When we learn to win over people and their confidence, then we can easily get into their brains and dominate them. And cunningness is the only thing that can help us do that.

Be cunning enough to understand strengths, weaknesses and interests of the people you know and people you meet. Show interest in what they like and what they don't, but do not show approval or dismal. This will set you up in the positive side of their mind. When they will think about you positively, domination will be easier.

Another thing is to not let yourself be dominated. We have already discussed this, but it is the perfect time to explore it more. You cannot let people dominate over you in a way or the other just because they are more accomplished than you. You simply cannot let your relatives tell you what to do. You cannot let your mother dictate some stories about your distant cousin who got into an Ivy League college and that you should get in, too. You simply cannot. But these stories and advices will only stop the day you will truly emerge out as a champion. What do you do till then?

Remember the chapter about anger? Quietly listen to and put every one of those stories and advice that people tell you in the anger repository to cash them later. Till then, keep some and let everyone say what they want. So, summing this one up in a line, dominate and don't get dominated.

You know, many follow every single thing written in this book. They are born as someone different, are meant to do different things. They live most of their life as genius.

But then, some real shit happens because of these two statements:

1. What will people say?
2. What will people think?

Yes, It is easy to say, 'be a rebel and screw everything else, don't listen what people say against you.' It is cool to say that, and you will be called a hipster for doing so, maybe. You must have found these lines in every other book, every other movie and every other song conveyed in different manners. But what we do is that we misinterpret these lines as 'Go immature, go bananas.'

These lines actually mean that most people you meet in life will not give you constructive criticism. Yes, some will genuinely try to help you, but most of them will try to corrupt your mind talking nonsense about life. They will keep going on, bragging things and telling you some things you shouldn't go for in your life.

'It is IMPRACTICAL. NO ONE can EVER do things like you are thinking. Why are you going for IMPOSSIBLE things? Are you NUTS?'

But, they will be the ones to lick your boots when you succeed in life. It is your body, your brain, your intelligence and your path. Never allow anyone to take control of it. Let them keep saying whatever they want to say. Let them keep thinking shit about you. Just work quietly and keep running. You don't physically need to shut their mouths. Just keep smiling whenever they say such things and tell yourself that you will prove these suckers wrong.

With this, remember not to follow the lines of 'Status Quo'. What is Status Quo? To define it simply, it is just 'The current state'. Status Quo is maintaining and keeping things just as the way they are presently. It is what keeps societies ticking along day in, day out. It's what keeps people going to work every day, children attending school, consumers consuming and pretty much any other standard every day activity you might think of. Well, it is fine. It is integral to keep a society moving along. But you're not a society. You're an individual, with personal hopes, belief and an infinitely complex persona.

The Status Quo doesn't care about who you are or what you want. Its job is to keep everything moving smoothly, by creating standardized humans who are born, go through the education system, marry, have kids, find jobs, pay taxes and retire when they're grey and too old to enjoy retirement. Yeah, the old school life that a majority lives, and dies living.

There's not much wiggle room when the Status Quo is watching over you. Unemployed because you're between jobs? *What a lazy oxygen thief!* Busy following your dreams? *Ugh, delusional moron!* Wearing bright red shoes? *Big-headed show off!* Stopped a stranger, told them they were beautiful? *Damn! What a creep!*

The Status Quo dulls you, drags you down and creates a living robot out of you. It never stops, even when you are an amorphous blob that is just coasting through life, going from one bill payment to another, never being content or finding true happiness, another cog in the system. What happens if you dare to step out of the Status Quo? It mostly causes a catastrophic world changing event, right?

Nope. That doesn't happen. What happens is this: you look back at the Status Quo you've abandoned and it is just the same as ever, carrying on like nothing has happened. You ask yourself why you even bothered conforming to the Status Quo all these years, if it even mattered. And the truth is, it didn't. The world is so big, that the effect of one person rerouting to the road less travelled is barely even felt.

All those times when you didn't do something you really wanted to, because it may have 'rocked the boat' or turned you into a social outcast, were for nothing, were opportunities missed for nothing.

Stepping out of the Status Quo to do what you want will nearly always be met with huge rewards. Look at the founders of the largest companies in the world and you will almost always find that none of them tend to follow the Status Quo. Society appreciates people who are different, who are unafraid of expressing what is in their minds and pursue their dreams. Society looks up to them as leaders that impact and mould the world we live in. Sure, people will gossip about you, envy you and even try to stop you from doing what you want. It's just the collective embrace of the Status Quo that is trying to hold you back. Ignore your critics and pursue your ideas, or live in regret of 'what could've been' and act like a champion.

But hold on, how can you do away with the Status Quo?

You have to live life on your terms, not on others' terms. It means that you must be the sole decider of your life path. Not your girlfriend, not your wife, not your parents, not the old lady down the street from where you live, or your dog. Only you can decide your life path.

There is another thing you need to know. You must have read many metaphors about life. Life is like a roller coaster, life is like a box of chocolates, life is like a bicycle, life is like bullshit – okay that one doesn't go well. The point is, life has been defined in many ways in literature. So, what is it exactly like? What is life? Or better still, what is life all about? Is it only about finding yourself?

This book isn't about philosophical stuff. It is about champions. I'll quote a champion here, 'Life isn't about finding yourself. Life is about creating yourself.' But George Bernard Shaw doesn't define life here, or does he?

He does.

Life is what you make of it. This sentence is really simple. You may have read it many times before. Think about it. You cannot spend your entire life finding yourself. Instead of finding yourself, start discovering your skills. Then comes the part we talked about till now: creating yourself, creating your identity, creating the man you are and you should be. Instead of spending a major part of your life looking for yourself, you can spend time making yourself.

Merely reading what is written in this chapter will not shape up your persona and give you a proper identity. Read, think, act. Grooming yourself internally is overlooked, but is really important. Having a distinct identity is the hallmark of a champion. Trust yourself and keep working on improving your skills and creating yourself.

Keep reading, champion.

Other Aspects

So far, we have talked about anger, pain, respect, belief, procrastination, sloth, hope and anxiety. We have also talked about yourself and others. Are we done with learning everything to become a champion? Do we have all the weapons in our arsenal? We have the major ones, but there are some smaller ones left. It is time to talk about them.

We have touched briefly on the issue of planning and plotting in the chapter about procrastination. We know what analysis paralysis means, and what happens when we over think what we want to do. We can sum it up as, if we just keep planning and don't do the work, things will never go our way. Notice how the word 'just' is written. The point is that mere planning will not lead us to our destination, but we cannot ignore the concept of planning. So here is the first small thing a champion does. **A champion plans.**

First, we need to understand the reason behind planning. Why should we plan if everything is clear in our brain?

You must know about Mike Tyson. Arguably the most popular boxer of the modern era, Tyson made over 300 million dollars being a boxer. He was treated as a legend and a badass. Then in 2003, he filed for bankruptcy. What happened? How can you have 300 million dollars and declare bankruptcy just like that? The reason was, Tyson had never planned. He never planned for the day he lost his balance in the ring. He ignored a simple fact: champions have bad days, but they must plan for those days.

When you have simple plans, you catapult yourself to a more advantageous situation than your peers. When you have a complete view of your intentions, you will be prepared to execute them and you will be more likely to flatten obstacles in your way. With planning, you break down things required to do for a job and then, you can work easily and efficiently.

There are small plans: the plans that you make to keep things going smoothly; and then there are big plans: your plans about life. Throughout this book, we have talked about the big plans. We have talked about success, about accomplishing things and about being a champion. By now, we have a clear idea of how to get what we want. The real deal now is how to plan for the small things. Before that, let us get into the types of small planning so that we have a general idea of this:

1. Haphazard planning: When you plan haphazardly, you wake up with a vague idea of what you intend to get done. You go through the day performing your tasks in whatever order you want, and do what feels

like the best thing to do at a given time. Haphazard planning needs no planner. Under this scheme, writing things down is pretty useless, as you will do whatever you feel like. This type of planning is at times lacks structure. Strangely, it works for some people.

2. Daily planning: This type of planning has more structure than haphazard planning, yet their day-to-day activities generally vary quite a lot. You cannot plan for more than a few days in advance at a time because every week is different. This type of planning is generally used by people with variable work hours, or whose lives are in a state of transition. The problem that exists is that you don't know what the next week will bring, but you can be sure enough of the next day or two.
3. Weekly planning: People under this scheme tend to have a much more fixed work schedule, and their lives are generally constant. The next week can be planned with ease as there will be little to no variation in their schedule.
4. Monthly planning: Under this scheme, either the person has an extremely fixed and constant life, or they are planning general dates rather than specific scheduling. This kind of planning is usually tough to catch up with as however constant and static your life is there will be some different days or weeks.

Now you have to determine what kind of planner you are. Nearly everyone uses a combination of all schemes. But, most people will be dominant in one or the other. The key is to use every scheme under different circumstances and for different reasons. Most of us are haphazard planners. There is no fault in that, but being a haphazard planner exclusively isn't good. You have to combine different types and then work on them.

The only problem we have now is to follow the plans. For this, you have to convince yourself that work will go easy on you if you stick to your plans. You need to acknowledge this fact. Following plans isn't that hard. All you have to do is keep going exactly as you planned to go. If you are someone who thinks that it is futile to take a pen and paper and etch out your schedule, make a mental plan of what you should do. Try haphazard planning. Either way, plan. Planning always gives great rewards. Planning is something that is associated only with champions, puny mortals don't plan.

Moving on, there is another thing we need to talk about. This is completely different from what we have talked about up until now.

You must have gone through various things in life. Some of them may have been embarrassing. We are talking about those memories which; when you remember, you cringe and think that you were really a sucker back then. The decisions you took in the past make you disappointed in yourself. Yes, we are talking about **regret**.

First of all, let us make this clear: escaping regret is hard. It will keep clinging on to you no matter how hard you try to throw it away. And it isn't your fault. This idea of living life with no regrets is impossible for all but one percent of human beings. People act like having regret is a burden that you carry around with you and so having regrets is bad. Well, that's dumb. If you have regrets, it only means you have a conscience, and you are smart enough to realize you've made bad decisions in the past. You are smart enough to know that the scars of the past that you are carrying are not to be cried about because they will be the reminders of your victory.

Martin Sheen once said, "The Irish tell the story of a man who arrives at the gates of heaven and he asks to be let in and St. Peter says, 'Of course. Show us your scars.' The man said, 'I have no scars.' St. Peter says, 'What a pity. Was there nothing worth fighting for?'"

So, it is perfectly normal to carry regret. But carrying regret and living in the past is different. A higher degree of regret makes you pity yourself for an entire lifetime. Regretting, just like analysis paralysis, wastes the time that you should be using to doing your work. Thinking about the past is one of the easiest ways to bring yourself down because it is always the horrible things that we remember most. It is always the bad things that we have done. What you have done in the past will only hurt you if you do it again. Make sure to tell yourself what you will never do again, and then tell yourself what you will do.

Firm your resolve, but base it on your courage and independence. Regret is good only for telling yourself what you will never do again. Once you know the things you will never do again, regret magically transforms into wisdom. And wisdom gives strength.

Everyone screws up many times in life. Champions screw up most, because they try most. But later, they do not look back with regret, because they know that those things brought them to the position they got to. Instead, they look back at those moments, smile, and tell themselves that they took many things from those moments, and that those moments taught them some real values. Here is a little story about the man we know as Mahatma Gandhi.

Mahatma Gandhi, the man admired by the entire world for his truthfulness and greatness had one of those moments in his life. When he was a young boy, Gandhi stole a piece of gold from his brother's armlet to clear a small debt of about Rs. 25. The debt wasn't even his own. The act became more than he could bear. The crime weighed down heavily on his heart and he kept thinking about it.

He made up his mind never to steal again. Now the real deal was that he wanted to confess the crime to his father, but didn't have the guts to do so. Nope, he wasn't afraid that he would get a beating because his father had never beaten any of his children. Gandhi was worried more about the pain that he would cause his father.

After a lot of thought, Gandhi decided that the risk should be taken. He wrote out the confession on a slip of paper and handed it to his father. In the note, he not only confessed to his guilt, but also asked to be punished for it. He closed the letter with a request to his father that he should not punish himself for his son's offence.

With trembling hands, Gandhi handed the confession to his father who was then suffering from a fistula and was confined to bed. Gandhi sat opposite his father on the small wooden plank that served as his father's bed. As he read the note, tears trickled down his father's cheeks, wetting the paper. For a moment he closed his eyes in thought and then tore up the note. He had sat up to read it. He again lay down. Mohandas also started crying. He could see the pain his father was going through.

According to Gandhi, this was one of those few moments that changed his life. He never wanted his father to cry, that too because of him. But he did not regret it. Instead, he learned from the incident. Today, he is remembered as a champion, is admired for his truthfulness, and is one of the key figures in history of not only India, but of the world.

It is true that *those* bad and embarrassing scenarios will keep popping up in your brain, and it is hard to get rid of them. But the problem will be doubled if you try to voluntarily forget all the scenarios.

Regretting and self-loathing will eat up your time as well as your brain. It is stupid to give time to regret rather than doing something productive. Only cowards live in the past, champions work for today and the future.

We all have the tendency to look towards the future. We try to look at what we can be. We try to look at what we want. We wonder what it will be like to get there. What you desire may be a great lifestyle. It may be a degree. It may be a new job. It may even be that girl you love.

The key is to amplify this tendency. Plan for the future and don't think about the past. What you need from your past is closure. You need what you have learnt from the mishaps and not the actual scenario. This will help you fend off regret.

You are on your path to become the hero of your own story. You may be going, or you may have already gone through your dark phase of life. Now you have to fight, every day, to get to where you want to be. It doesn't mean that you should fight against yourself and loathe yourself for things you have done in your past. It means to work your way to a better self and fight against all forces that might hold you back - naysayers, bad habits, 'not wanting to do it' and so on.

You are writing your story, a story of your journey to become a champion. Wouldn't it be a damn boring story if there were no challenges to overcome? Do you think Karate Kid would have been a movie that anyone would have liked to watch if the success was pre-written, if the main character didn't have to work his way out of failure and misery?

Of course, there is one thing that movies don't show us: how to keep one's motivation levels up. How does one do all the work that is necessary for success? There are cut scenes that jump over the hard parts, while in reality the hard parts are the ones that feel the longest and toughest. That is what you have read in this book so far. You know how to keep yourself up. Now you just need to remember that one thing: You will get there. Hard work will pay off. Every day, move one step forward. If you manage to do two or three, that is great, but the only thing that is important is that you do at least one step. Every day.

Then you will see how the main character - you - becomes the hero; how the past shaped the way you think; how the past shaped the way you behave. But how it doesn't shape who you will become - because that is what you will decide now. Remember that there will never be a greater moment than the one you are about to live. Conquer it, and do not give a damn to regrets.

In the first chapter, we talked about turning anger and pain into something productive by channeling them. We also talked a bit about how we can turn vices into something useful. Is there any exception to that? Yes. **Fear**.

Why can't fear be used just like we use anger and pain? It can be a motivator, right? Nope. Fear isn't like anger, selfishness or pain. Anger and pain can be trusted, but fear is always a backstabber. Anger and pain are meant to be used to reach our goals, while fear is an obstacle on the way to our goals. It will always try to pull you down and make you stop doing your work. It is an utterly negative and bitter feeling that shouldn't have any place in a champion's life. But of course, it doesn't go that easy.

It is always fear that holds you back from doing something. The most common form is the fear of failure. There are many others. Everyone has his own particular type of fear. And everyone knows that fear stops them from doing many things they could have done. It invades like a terminal cancer and takes over from your core being. Most of the time, it turns you coward and afraid, very afraid.

There have been many things written and said over fighting fear. But can it really be fought? You cannot remove or overcome fear by fighting it; for as long as you fight it, you give it more power and control. You give it all your strings. It will keep growing as long as you think of it as an adversary or an enemy to be or overcome.

Champions do not fight fear. They rise above, and move beyond it. You can learn to move beyond it by understanding that fear is only a thought or belief that you hold both in your conscious and unconscious belief system. It is just a passing thought that will feed on you and grow powerful if you think about and fuel it.

You give rise to fear. You tell yourself to get scared of something. And then, by fighting it, you make it more real and powerful. That is the mistake most people make. That is not the answer to overcome fear. The answer lies in the realization and self-actualization that you created fear as a reaction to external circumstances, and only you can eliminate it, but not by fighting it. If you try to fight it, then you are just fighting with yourself. You are fighting in your own mind with your own creation.

A champion knows that there will always be circumstances that may give rise to fear, but he immediately calms his mind so that the emotion of fear never rises up and takes control. He doesn't allow it to dominate. He is not fighting it back but rather, he just takes control of his mind and remains in control of his emotions, instead of letting his emotions control him.

This is where most people fail. They allow their emotions to control them. They don't learn to control their own mind.

What we are trying to learn here is not to fight fear, but instead remain in control of our own mind so that fear never even comes up. For if you start fighting fear, you have already lost. You are telling fear that it is worth of your time and energy. You have already given fear more power and control than it deserves to have in your mind.

Think of the difference between a professional lion tamer entering a cage where there are lions, versus an average person entering the same cage.

The lion tamer is not afraid, he is not fighting back his fear because he doesn't have any fear. He eliminated it in his training to become a lion tamer. He learned early in his training that if the lions smell any fear, he is dead. So *he* controls and dominates the situation, not the lions. He controls the situation because he controls his mind. He knows that if fear enters his mind, he loses his control and power. If he fights fear, he has lost control and power to his fear.

To even enter into battle with the fear in your mind, you have lost. Because you are now using precious mental resources to fight back the fear when instead you should be using your mental resources to quickly analyze, figure out, navigate and control the situation that is in front of you.

If the average person walks into the cage that has lions, and tries to fight back his fear, even if he pretends and appears not to have any fear, the lions will still smell his fear and attack. He was doomed before he even walked into the den of lions because he had not trained himself to quiet his mind and eliminate his fear first before walking into battle.

When others see that you are not in fear as you face a fearful situation, they are in awe. When your enemy sees that you are not afraid, he begins to have doubts. He wonders why you are smiling in spite of all the situations and you can then overcome him more easily because you are more self-confident than him. This is how you must train your mind, so that whenever a potentially scary situation comes up you can quickly take control of it. If you learn how to do this, fear will never even have a chance to rise up and control you.

Always remember that you are a beast and this puny, trivial thing called fear cannot control you and your actions. Keep reminding yourselves that you hold all the strings. Also, stop fearing fear. Remember that you cannot let a mere feeling take control of your life. Just like fear, there is another thing that is our creation, and stops us from doing what we want to do. It seems trivial, but most of the times it is the one that creates most of the problems. That thing is **excuse**.

Each one of us has made an excuse at some point in our lives as to why we don't want to do something that deep down we know we should.

We keep telling ourselves and the people, 'It's too cold outside to go for a walk.' 'I'm going to fail this exam anyways so why bother studying?' or probably the most common 'I just don't feel like it.'

How are we going to push past that now? Excuses and throwing blame are the same way of saying, 'I'm not in control.' Well we know that not being in control of yourselves totally sucks. Excuses feel good temporarily, but don't be fooled, they can only hurt you. So how should we overcome and get rid of our excuses?

There is something strange about excuses. Though they inflict a lot of damage, they don't put up much of a fight. If you try to combat them, you can usually succeed and that too easily. But that isn't the only thing. If you defeat your excuse once, and then twice, it will never strike the third time.

You only have to beat it twice. Why? Because once you beat an excuse one time, it will try to pop up again once in your mind. When you thrash it the second time, you can tell it to get its ass off your mind and it will do that. The second beating puts a seal to the fact that it will never bother you again, because it cannot survive in the mind of a champion.

Now comes the main part, how to do it? And the answer is, *just do it.* This isn't a strategic Nike's marketing campaign, but the real answer to stop making excuses is that simple. Just do it.

Yes. No pompous sentences here. No long rants about some special tricks to fend excuses. Only three words: just do it.

Keep telling yourself these three words every time you make an excuse. You know you want to do it, but you still keep making these excuses because you have forced them onto yourself somehow. Remember that if your brain starts making a tiny excuse, the minute you start thinking about that excuse a thousand irrational excuses will be bred. The key here is not to give your brain any time to breed excuses. Just tell yourself your work, and then just do it. Force the excuse back and ask it to get the hell out of your brain.

But what happens when we face an excuse that actually has some strength behind it? When we face an excuse that has the potential to convince us to stop our work? It is at that point we can set priorities. If we're doing something that we honestly feel takes priority over the next thing, then we're doing the most important thing, which is the main goal. After the first task is done, we can move onto the next without guilt.

Charles Bukowski, the great American poet wrote, 'Baby, air and light and time and space, have nothing to do with it and don't create anything except maybe a longer life to find; new excuses for.'

It is interesting to note that the same guy has 'Don't try' written on his epitaph. Why did Bukowski contradict the lines he wrote? Just give up and don't do anything? That is one defeatist attitude. But then, how does someone become a successful writer with that kind of a mantra? The thing is that, most of us misread the intent. In an interview with Bukowski's wife she explains it simply as 'Don't try, just do'.

Trying can be an excuse. 'Why isn't that done yet? Well, I am trying!'

'I am trying' sounds like we are actively working at something when we may not be. It makes us sound like a sore loser who cannot do his job properly. It's an excuse that will stop us from actually doing the work. To tell yourself that you are just trying will not motivate you, instead it will push you into Utopia. It will give you a false reasoning that you are actually doing your work. Trying is a bad excuse. Screw trying. Just Do. You know you can, just tell yourself you will.

You know that moment. That moment of failure. That moment when you didn't get to the finish line, didn't pass the exams, didn't impress the girl or guy, and let your parents down. You had your chances, but you told yourself that they didn't matter, that there would be other goddamn chances. You told yourself that you were tired. You took a break when it wasn't needed.

And late at night, alone in the dark, when faced with a set of circumstances you can't see your way out of, you wonder about what might have been. You should have pushed yourself harder. You should have made it happen. You should have ignored the fear and done it, done it better than your half-assed attempt, done more than good enough and hoped you would get by.

Well, now, there you are. You know you need to do more. You need to run harder, work longer, think smarter. You know that you have to dig deeper and around more corners than you thought you have to. The facts of life are spelled out for you, as clear as day, with one clear rule: No more excuses. Do not go after what you think you should, but what you know you must. Get going.

If we divide the types of people on the basis of their wants, there are two:

The first type has a clear idea of what it takes to be a champion, that is, including the total cost and sacrifices it will require to get there. The second type says they know they want to be champion, but have this in mind as some sort of 'it would be awesome I become someone like that!'

The former fixate on their own goals and go chasing after them like a shark. The latter look at the successful, the accomplished, and ask themselves how on earth they do it, as if they have some sort of cheat code and they are just lucky. This is the type that would like to begin a lemonade stand, but then objects that they don't have the knowledge about lemons or an idea of where to start. Bullshit. If you really wanted it, you would be a walking freaking encyclopedia on lemonades, because you'd spent every waking minute researching online and getting in touch with those in the know.

Just take a moment and look at the people around you, stuck in minimum-wage job with the desire to become rich or famous, but then don't put in the work, because they see some sort of obstacles everyday: a lack of time, money, or whatever. Now look at all the champions, working 100-hour weeks, turning obstacles into opportunities and their dreams into reality. While normal people dream about success, the champions wake up and chase it.

People keep saying 'I want this' or 'I want that' but '(insert lame excuse here)'. If you want something, go get it. If you want to do something, just do it. As J. Michael Straczynski puts it, people spend too much time finding other people to blame, too much energy finding excuses for not being what they are capable of being, and not enough energy putting themselves on the line, growing out of the past, and getting on with their lives.

A champion can never try to reason with excuses. A champion despises excuses. Think about reasons to do your work instead of thinking about excuses. There are infinitely many excuses and infinitely many reasons. Stop looking for excuses and start looking for reasons. Excuses aren't worth to be thought upon. They are to be thrown away.

Along with excuses, there is something else a champion has no place in life for. And that is, complaining. The act of complaining has been around for a long time. It has brought nothing but negativity to the people committing the act and those who have to listen to it. Complaining about your problems does nothing but bring you and others down. It makes you look weak, lost, and pathetic.

You know that there are many toxic people around you who may fill you with a plethora of negative thoughts. The problem with removing those toxic people from your life is that you may be one of them, if you are a chronic complainer. 'Oh, I couldn't do this thing because some little obstacle came in my way.' 'I could have done if I had some more resources!' Oh, rubbish. That is nothing but complaining.

If you have realized that you have been complaining by observing your behaviors and reflecting on them, then it shouldn't be too hard to fix this issue. It is an easy issue to fix as long as you are willing to put forth the effort and actually want to change. Here are two of the steps:

1. Monitor yourself: Continue analyzing your behavior and words to see when and why you are complaining. Don't be too self-aware, instead, focus on those moments when it strikes you that you are going slightly overboard. Monitor what you are complaining about, and then find the root cause of the problem. Stress on why you were complaining, and if it was because of lack of something, think if your work could be done without that thing or if there is any other way to do it.
2. Reflect: Every night before you go to sleep, reflect on what you have said and done that day. Because reflecting will help you refrain from complaining. Self-reflection is pretty important. It removes all the toxic feelings and excuse off your body when you start reflecting your thoughts.

Now there must be a question in your brain. Is complaining really that bad? The answer to this is a resounding yes. It may seem harmless, but it makes you look weak and vulnerable. It can alter your path to become a champion greatly. You see, the truth is that people don't care about your problems as much as you may think. When you complain, people will either try to give you unsolicited advice to feed their own ego because they love to be right, or they will just pity you. A champion doesn't let anyone pity him, never. Neither does he go around telling the world that he could not accomplish something because he had some obstacles. A champion just does his work. And that is what you should do instead of making excuses and complaints; just do it.

We have discussed the relationship between two entirely different qualities in the book, and we have discussed qualities misunderstood and taken out of context. But a champion needs to know one more thing which is predominantly unclear to others: the difference between **discipline and motivation**.

Let us take both these terms one by one. What is discipline? Discipline is abiding by a particular goal and following steps to achieve it. Imagine that you have a long journey ahead to a place called success, and you are travelling by a boat all by yourself. Discipline is rowing the boat. Now what is motivation? Motivation is the spark you need to move ahead. Motivation is the wind in your sails.

If all you do is row, you'll get tired and be burnt out. If you just rely on the wind blowing in the right direction, you won't get very far. But if you use both, you will surely reach the destination. Champions row their boats a bit differently though: they create their own wind. They understand and manage their emotions to a degree where they can make themselves feel the energy of motivation. They can pull themselves out of a storm by both rowing and altering the wind, by both discipline and motivation.

How to create your own wind now? Here are some steps you can follow:

1. Managing your brain's moods: Often, we find ourselves in a bad mood for one reason or another. This can kill motivation to do anything. It's especially bad if the negative mood is caused by feeling discouraged within the very sphere you're trying

to improve. A negative mood increases mental access to negative things. This is how we go on a downward spiral. We can counter this by consciously identifying and focusing on positive aspects of our environment or day, effectively stopping the spiral. Think of all the good things that are happening or will happen to you. The more we practice this, the easier it gets. It is a simple thing, but difficult to master.

2. Know: Know that you can create your own wind. When you start believing that you can easily motivate yourself for your tasks, you will turn into an unstoppable force.

3. Willpower: The more we use our willpower, the stronger it gets. This is a real thing. So while rowing can be very difficult, by refusing to row or believing that the wind is what you need to do stuff, you are literally refusing to become stronger. Remember that motivation gives you willpower points. Discipline costs willpower points. Get those points and use them.

4. Framing: You can reframe setbacks as opportunities and failures as a list of lessons learned. Frame every failure as things you learnt from. Often, people experience bursts of motivation. 'I am going to change my life. I'll do things differently. I'll start developing a new skill!' But soon, the shine comes off the apple, the wind dies, and, well, they stop. Their motivation wasn't inside, but driven by the novelty of it all. Champions recognize when this

happens, and counter it by consciously finding new things to appreciate. They find new takes on their old task. Sometimes they can even connect back with their original mindset when things were new and special, putting something that has become boring into a favorable context. This counter is doubly good because it encourages you to learn new approaches to things.

Motivation is what starts the car and discipline is what keeps it running on that thousand miles road trip to the goal. They go hand in hand. Discipline is what keeps you doing the thing after you've lost your motivation. Sometimes motivation will fail, and only discipline will keep you on the path. Sometimes discipline will fail, and motivation will keep you from jumping off the path. The point is that both will always support each other.

You just have to manage and let both of them work in sync. The key is to have a good, personal discipline paired up with a lot of motivation. When you will follow your codes and motivate yourself on your journey, the results will be extraordinary. Keep yourself up with discipline and motivation.

If you really want both of them in an instant for doing something, the answer is simple: **challenge yourself** to get that thing. When you start challenging yourself for something, discipline and motivation willingly get along. There is nothing wrong in challenging yourself. When you challenge yourself, you actually are getting challenged by someone who knows your weaknesses and strengths, and in turn improve them. Don't believe it? Let us read a story about a guy called Jim.

Jim grew up in a family that was so poor that for a time, they lived in their van on a relative's lawn. In his early years at school, he was very quiet and didn't have many friends. He was an undiagnosed dyslexic, and often struggled in school. But he believed in his future even when it may have seemed likely he would follow his parents in poverty.

From a young age, Jim knew that he had a greater calling to follow. He wanted to become a performer. A comic! When he was just 10, he even mailed his resume to The Carol Burnett Show. He was rejected, but that sense of hope continued as Jim got older.

Time passed but Jim never even smelled success. One night in 1990 when he was a struggling young comic trying to make his way in Los Angeles, he climbed to the top of a hill. While sitting there, broke, looking down over the city, and dreaming of his future, he wrote himself a fake check for $10 million, put in the notation line 'for acting services rendered,' and dated it for Thanksgiving 1995.

He stuck that check in his wallet and that fake check triggered both his discipline and motivation. He worked hard for the next five years - and the rest, as they say, is history.

By 1995, Jim Carrey had seen the tremendous success of Ace Ventura, Pet Detective, The Mask and Liar, Liar. His per film fee at that point had escalated to $20 million.

Challenging yourself will always yield great results. When you do this, you give yourself a particular target that you wish to hit in a time interval. You become the boss as well as the employee; you become the one man company.

Now when everything will be given in your hands, all you will do is direct yourself to the target and hit it. That is the beauty of challenging yourself.

You know most of the things about motivation. What about discipline? Can discipline be triggered like, DISCIPLINE MODE ON! Nope.

What you need to know is that discipline is a process, not an innate quality.

When you fail in your discipline, it's not an indicator of some intrinsic fault in you, it's an indicator of a fault in your process. To use a concrete example, imagine you were building an engine, and near the end of the process, you realized you forgot a critical piece. While rebuilding it with the missing piece, you then forget a different piece. Oh goddamn it! How frustrating!

Would that be an indicator that you were incapable of building an engine, or that the engine was unbuildable? Of course not! You'd take the engine apart until you could put in the missing piece, and then continue the process.

If you ran into a stumbling block you couldn't get past, you might read a book on building engines or talk to a qualified mechanic. You might take a break from the project and then come back to it with a fresh perspective, and that's fine, too.

If you were building an engine for the first time, would you expect yourself to be able to do it perfectly on the first try?

So, don't expect to succeed at discipline immediately. Being unkind to yourself is counterproductive; telling yourself that you are stupid or bad or weak doesn't build the engine. Examining the process, making sure you have the tools and parts you need and recognizing places you can improve your process will help you make the engine.

Do not look at your mistakes as an indicator of an intrinsic fault. They are a step in learning the skill of discipline. The fact that you want to learn this skill shows great promise for actually learning it. Also, remember to keep up motivation and discipline, and let them complement each other.

By now, we have covered all big and small aspects left. We have covered all the melee weapons a champion needs. Just remember to plan, do not let regret overshadow you, don't fear, stop giving excuses, keep discipline and motivation in synchronization, and live like a champion. These things are summed up in a single chapter because they do not require a lot of efforts, they just require mental strength.

Contrary to conventional wisdom a war is not won in one battle. A war is won by many small courageous and skillful acts. Weapons are forged. Plans are made. Miles are marched. Then the battle follows. And maybe, just maybe a second or a third before the final victory is achieved.

What you are doing now is, you are fighting a war. You cannot expect that one day or one decision can make your dreams become reality. You need to forge weapons - learn, build character, develop your body and mind. You need to plan - look ahead and see which steps you need to take, which people you need to meet and which challenges you need to win. Then, you need to march, no matter how tired your mind and legs grow. Without the march, without the hard and breath-taking miles all the preparation was for nothing.

And if you have done all this - there will be a battle, a challenge unlike any other. You will have to be strong. You will have to be enduring. And you will have to use all your willpower to win this battle. This might be the end. You may get really tired during the war. You may start thinking everything just sucks and you should stop this shit right away. But if you just hold on, you will win. You will emerge as a champion.

The sweet victory will be worth every dropping tear or pearl of sweat. Your ancestors fought their battles and risked their lives. They risked those lives for you, to create a future that you could live. And now it is up to you, it is up to you to follow your ancestors.

Plan, stop regretting, don't fear, stop giving excuses, keep discipline and motivation with you, and never accept a world of limitations and self-pity.

Put on your boots, champion, and start writing your story.

Hello, Champion

In 1938, an army man from Hungary called Karoly Takacs was the top pistol shooter in the world. He was expected to win the gold in the 1940 Olympic Games scheduled for Tokyo.

The expectations vanished one terrible day, just months before the Olympics. While training with his army squad, a hand grenade exploded in Takacs' right hand, and Takacs' shooting hand was blown off. Yes, blown off.

Takacs spent a month in the hospital depressed at both the loss of his hand and the end to his Olympic dream.

Hold on right there.

Isn't this the point when most people quit? Isn't this the point from when they spend the rest of their life feeling sorry for themselves and seek attention?

Most people would have quit, but not Takacs. Takacs was a champion. Champions know that they can't let circumstances keep them down. They understand that life is hard and that they can't let life beat them down.

Yes, Takacs did the unthinkable. He picked himself up, dusted himself off, and decided to learn how to shoot with his left hand. His left goddamn hand! Instead of focusing on what he didn't have, that is, a world class right shooting hand, he decided to focus on what he did have: incredible mental toughness. He kept practicing.

In the Spring of 1939 he showed up at the Hungarian National Pistol Shooting Championship. Other shooters approached Takacs to give him their fake condolences and to congratulate him on having the strength to come watch them shoot. They were surprised when he said, 'I didn't come to watch, I came to compete.'

And you know what hit them hard? *Takacs won.*

The 1940 and 1944 Olympics were cancelled because of World War II. It looked like Takacs' Olympic Dream would never have a chance to realize itself. But Takacs kept training and in 1944 he qualified for the London Olympics.

At the age of 38, Takacs won the Gold Medal and set a new world record in pistol shooting. Four years later, Takacs won the Gold Medal again at the 1952 Helsinki Olympics.

Do not, I repeat, do not try to make yourself feel inspired again. This story is here to showcase you what a champion does: he conquers life.

We have talked about it all: the ups and downs, the good and the bad, everything. We have talked upon our arsenal of weapons to reach our goals. We have talked about the obstacles and hindrances. We have talked about every quality a champion possesses. Well, is that it?

Can merely reading these lines make you a champion? Nope. These lines are here to tell you what you are expected to do as a champion. They are meant to fill you with everything you need. But the implementation is entirely up to you. Me, your parents, girlfriend or boyfriend, husband or wife, anyone cannot kick you off your couch and make you work for your dreams. It is you who has to do this. It is you who will make your future self. It is you, champion.

The point is that you shouldn't just read this book, charge yourself up for a while and then throw whatever you got from this book away in the days that follow. The point is to understand everything and keep working.

Somewhere deep inside your brain there are two voices competing with each other. One wants you to follow what is written in this book and start working at this very moment, other is telling you that this is all bullshit, and you must go check your Facebook, Instagram some photos or watch television. The only problem is, because of some technical reasons, the latter voice is louder. But it can be shut up if you tell it to do so, sternly.

What are you waiting for, champion? Go ahead. Shut that voice up. Fill in the rage, everything you have and give the best damn shot towards your goal. Don't let depressing thoughts get to you. Remember, life is knocking you down so that when you stand up again, your punch has twice the power of a normal punch. Let life play its tricks on you. You keep smiling, and keep doing what you are meant to do.

You are headed towards many great and wonderful things. There's no doubt that you're soon going to enjoy the fruits of your labor, being the next best version that you imagine that you can become. But as you've found, as we continue to find, it's only you who makes it happen. You are the boat in a turbulent ocean. What you must do is, apply some force and navigate your boat through the storm. Don't let the ocean take you some place you don't know. Take control and steer. You are larger than you think you are. You are everything that you admire, everything that you think you can become, and everything that you currently detest about yourself. You're all of it.

By now, you have understood that each of us gets the same choices, the same options and opportunities. We are all born into the unknown with an unlimited amount of potential and abilities. As we grow up, somewhere along the way, we decide to either be a champion or be a loser.

Yet, the amazing thing about choices is that we can change them along the way. Wrong choices are never final, and they can be fixed. They are not laws carved into stone, but words handwritten in sand. This is why, no matter where you are right now, no matter what your finances may be, what caste or creed you are, where you live, your last name, your health, your weight, anything that you think is holding you back really isn't. It is the choice to hold yourself back what is really holding you back. Letting the train of thought that somehow you will always fail to take command, by expecting the worst when the best is a possibility.

The time to choose to be a champion is now, not tomorrow. Decide to own up to your own potential. Decide to simply stop living the life that you don't want and start living the life that you want. Be a champion. Be yourself. Be the ultimate expression of your own potential. Expect the best, and prepare for the worst, because you are a champion. You will survive.

You may think you are not a champion. You may reason yourself into downgrading your potential, but let me tell you something: just making it to the point where you are in life, no matter how bad it may seem to you, is enough evidence that you are, indeed, a survivor.

Champions always survive. They always manage to get things done and they don't wait for the darkness to go away. They simply own up to their potential and move forward. Do not stop simply because you are scared. Fear is just the loser in you trying to keep you back. Do not buy in to it, because the rewards for courage are far greater than any fake safety provided by fear.

There must be a corner in your house that qualifies as your favorite corner. There must be a corner where you try to work your ass off to get your job done. It may be the desk in your room. A chair in your balcony, a space on the rooftop or anywhere else at your place. Promise yourself that one day, you will sit in that corner, thinking about everything you did there, every plan you made, all the work you did and feel glad about it. There may even be a place where you were insulted by people. A place you despise. Promise yourself that one day, you will visit that place, look at everyone around you bowing at your greatness, and smile at them. Promise that one day you will laugh at every asshole on earth who teased and mocked you. Promise to be a legend.

You just finished reading an entire book. You invested several hours of your life, but for what? Motivation? Not exactly. Everything you have read in this book is plain and simple fact and nothing else. This book was simply meant to help you discover the champion in you. This book is meant to inspire you to get off your couch and work. This book is meant to help you get what you want, and make your life worth living.

Remember, watching the 'one minute video that will change your life' or some motivational speaker blabbering about 'following your dreams' will not change your life. You will. You may feel pumped, but the point is to remain pumped up all the time. Take things personally. Your failures, victories and everything else. Be ruthless, be a barbarian and with that, be a thinker to reach your goals.

Oh, and yes. The time will come when you will ask yourself, 'Is everything really worth it?'

The thing that precedes this question is a failed attempt at something else. You might be trying to score great grades in your high school, or start a business, or may be working to land a job with your dream company. Regardless of what event precedes the question, the moment when the question arises – is when the real battle begins.

This is the moment where life actually calls you out into the arena for a fight. This will not be an ordinary fight. It will be a street fight. No rules, no referee, no count outs. Whoever walks out of that arena first will win.

Obviously the timing is always going to suck. You will be weaker, less confident and quite possibly afraid. All of the positive reinforcement techniques that you learnt so far are going to feel absolutely worthless – and now you get to play David before Goliath. There is nowhere to run once you're inside that arena, nothing to hide behind – no way to escape what waits for you once that door closes. Many before you have gone into that arena and not all of them have returned.

And you walk to that arena knowing this, fully aware that what you're about to engage in has been happening since man first walked the earth, yet you will take no solace in this. Even the fact that most have returned from the arena and returned stronger will bring you no relief. If you're lucky there will be one or two folks in your corner to help you, probably the people who love you, probably your parents. But they can't go into the arena with you, but you know they will be waiting for you when you come out. For some of you, that will be all you need to be victorious. Knowing that someone is waiting outside that door will give you exactly what you need to be the first out of the arena.

For others, there won't be anyone waiting when you emerge from that arena. Your trip has been deemed to be the more arduous, more difficult. Life has singled you out especially, I guess the assumption is with nothing to fight for, you simply won't fight. Life is expecting you to walk into that arena and succumb to whatever happens and do it without protest. Yes, sometimes this will not be a fair fight.

Whether you have someone waiting for you or not, what happens inside the arena doesn't change. You will have a decision to make and it will be a clear and profound decision. You will either go blow for blow with life in that arena or you will lose. There is no grey area here. This one is black and white. The Champion takes all.

Remember, you are not the first and you will not be the last. This trip to the arena is simply part of the price you pay to have what you want and become who you are meant to be: a champion. Do not run away from the arena. Step into it. This is where you decide to separate yourself – this is where you cement your legacy and your future. This arena is the place from where you will emerge a champion. Enter it. Everyone, your enemies, friends and the entire world is waiting for you to come out of the arena. They want to shake your hands and tell you those two words.

Hello, champion.